The Charm
of the Red Rose

✕

A Moral Explanation
of the Battle of Karbala

Abolqasem Fanaei

Preface by
Mohammad Jafar Amir Mahallati

Translated by
Elham Farahani

Edited by
Hasan Shikoh

Published in the United Kingdom by Sajjadiyya Press, 60 Weoley
Park Road, Selly Oak, Birmingham, B29 6RB.

Copyright 2025 by Sajjadiyya Press.
ISBN 978-1-9998621-0-7 (paperback)

A catalogue record for this book is available from the British
Library.

TABLE OF CONTENTS

TRANSLATOR'S PREFACE

As a Muslim girl, I grew up loving Imam Hussein deeply, yet the many interpretations of his martyrdom left me unsettled. Was his death simply God's will? If so, shouldn't we judge his killers less harshly? These questions stayed with me until I read Dr. Abolqasem Fanaei's The Charm of the Red Rose: A Moral Explanation of the Battle of Karbala in Farsi. Dr. Fanaei sees Karbala as a bold stand for moral principles—a view that struck a chord with me. Imam Hussein's refusal to accept humiliation inspired me most, driving me to share this profound work with English readers.

In a world needing cross-cultural understanding and moral clarity, this translation feels timely. Set in 680 CE, Karbala speaks to timeless struggles: resisting oppression, preserving dignity, and living virtuously amid hardship. Dr. Fanaei casts Imam Hussein as a role model for all—beyond Muslim or Shia boundaries—urging us to embrace values that connect us. I hope this translation shares that wisdom globally.

Translating this book was a heartfelt journey, weaving my reverence for Imam Hussein with the task of preserving Dr. Fanaei's philosophical insight. I've worked to make it clear and relatable for all readers. My deep thanks go to Dr. Fanaei for entrusting me with this honour. May this translation reflect his vision and inspire you to see Imam Hussein's legacy as a call to your own moral journey.

Elham Farahani
Assistant Professor of Applied Linguistics
Arak University, Iran, April 2025

The theories of two contemporary thinkers, Iris Murdoch and David Cook, raise two key and anxiety-inducing questions in the context of contemporary Imam Hussein Studies. Murdoch believes that in general, contemporary cultures focus on ethics and normative doctrines as crisis-oriented or what she calls 'quandary ethics'; that is, people only turn to ethical doctrines to resolve crises in their personal or social lives (Wadell, 1990). Otherwise, they do not care about ethical concerns. Now, a Shi'a Muslim can ask himself whether the teachings and school of Imam Hussein (may peace be upon him) are primarily concerned with addressing crises such as the removal of oppression in their daily life, or whether they can also serve as a reference and source of guidance beyond crises, and towards moral perfection.

David Cook, a contemporary martyrdom scholar, has also got an interesting observation regarding the approach of Islamic denominations towards the phenomenon of martyrdom. He states that for Ahl al-Sunnah wal-Jamā'a, that is the Sunni schools of Islam, martyrdom is seen as a happy phenomenon, while for Shi'as, it is regarded as a sorrowful event. As a result, Shi'as consider the martyrdom of their Imam as a subject of historical mourning. However, the martyrdom of Imam Hussein, who carries the honorific epithet as 'the master of all martyrs' and his companions, which is the subject of extensive mourning rituals in the Shi'a world, plays a significant role in shaping the identity of the Shi'a community (Cook, 2007). This creates a paradox where the martyrdom of Imam Hussein, in a forced battle with the Umayad caliph

Yazīd ibn Muʿawia (680 CE), is both a necessary component of Shiʿa historical identity and a matter of lamentation. Can this sorrowful identity be justified and defended?

In other words, if hypothetically, we imagine that Imam Hussein and his companions had not been martyred, the identity we know today in the Shiʿa world would have had a different form, content, and meaning; in which case, would the Shiʿas see the tragedy of ʿAshura as historically incidental? Or conversely, do they simply consider it necessary to highlight the highest examples of self-sacrifice and martyrdom? In short, can martyrdom be considered as simultaneously a mournful incident and an identity-making?

These questions also encompass a set of other questions: From the perspective of which ethical school does the tragedy and sacrifice of Karbala find its best form and meaning? Which ethical systems, such as consequentialism, deontologism, virtue ethics, formalism, rights-based ethics, religious ethics (divine command or Sharīʿah-oriented), etc. can better explain this tragedy and sacrifice? To what extent is the mourning philosophy in the history of Shiism a tool and to what extent is it authentic and essential? In the tragedy of Karbala, are two individuals facing each other on opposing political camps, or are they two different theological schools – one representing Imam Hussein and the other Yazīd? In this confrontation, where does the historical equation of power, justice, and rationality stand? What lessons does the incident of Karbala teach us from the perspectives of violence studies, ethics of war and peace? What are the consequences of changing and transforming analytical perspectives on this event from customary intellectual rationality to emotional, religious, ritualistic, and jurisprudential ethics? What meaning, message, and outcome does the tragedy of Karbala hold in the equation of relationships between life, dignity, and freedom?

There are several ways to provide answers to the above questions. The first is through referring to the prophetic tradition (*sirah*) and statements of Imam Hussein and his companions during the incident of Karbala. Second, it is through the posthumous analyses of Imam Hussein scholars and 'Ashura scholars relying on various ethical and historical theories.

Importantly, this book falls into the category of Imam Hussein studies that serves scholars facing complex moral questions in the contemporary world. It therefore is very timely, offering unique answers and insights into some of the above questions. The main motivation of Imam Hussein studies for the contemporary world is, firstly, to ensure that the personality of the Imam and his teachings are not confined solely to the tragedy of Karbala. Secondly, it aims to make both the overall teachings, and the teachings derivations thereof, from the tragedy and sacrifices of Karbala a guiding light for present and future generations.

The present work in the Persian language appears as a special issue in a series published annually by the Shiraz Majd Institute serving various scholars with interest in Islamic Peace Studies. The edited series tackle the tragedy of Karbala from the political, economic, psychological, sociological, legal and moral philosophy perspectives. In its English translation however, the present work on its own can be studied as an independent scholarship that helps an analytical view of the 'Ashura tragedy and a critical perspective of Yazīd's political system from a moral stance.

As I have frequently alluded to in my introductions to the Persian language series, if Imam Hussein's teachings are examined from the perspective of the ethics of war and peace, especially the comparative warfare ethics, it yields new and astonishing results, which are worthy of consideration by peacebuilders and future-studies scholars.

The present book, written by Abolqasem Fanaei, is important for several reasons. First, it provides a different perspective on the ethical and biographical analysis of Imam Hussein from the viewpoint of a moral philosophy. As a result, it sheds light on new dimensions of the teachings of Imam Hussein and highlights his profound moral contributions. Through a morally critical lens focused on the Karbala tragedy, Fanaie explores the relationship between power, justice, rationality, dignity and freedom. Moreover, Fanaie highlights the fine demarcation between the legalistic Sharī'ah-centred and ethical approaches, which contributes to the global dissemination of the teachings of Karbala and its heroes as moral exemplars. While sensitive to the fallacy of *anachronism,* Fanaie provides the religious intellectuals and neo-Mu'tazilite inclinations a valuable source of intellectual nourishment. Its relevance extends to recent controversial discussions regarding the relationship between religion and power.

The ethical analyses in this book which are focused on the triad of fear-centric, greed-centric, and freedom-centric religiosity, provides the readers with assistance in confronting the challenges discussed by contemporary German Egyptologist, Jan Assmann. According to Assmann, one of the most significant cultural tensions in history is the tension between polytheistic religions, including Greek and Egyptian religions, and

Abrahamic monotheistic religions that do not tolerate any other deity besides the one supreme God (Assmann, 2018).

Assmann believes that the concept of "exclusivity" in monotheistic perspectives inherently carries the potential for nurturing violence. However, some other contemporary European thinkers have arrived at different ways of attributing the causes of violence to ideologies. For example, Hannah Arendt (1970), Slavoj Žižek (2008) and Byung-Chul Han (2018) consider ideologies as causes of positive violence. A Muslim political philosopher may argue that there is no need to take a circuitous route in tracing the roots of social and political violence. For this, it may be sufficient to examine the theories of one of the most important and influential Muslim political philosophers, Abu al-Ḥasan al-Māwardī (d. 350 AH), to see how a despotic ruler, solely through military power, and no other merit, achieves legitimacy and control over an Islamic community in order to establish security (al-Māwardī, 2018). In contrast to the aforementioned ideology, one of the distinctions of traditional Shiʿa political philosophy is the emphasis on the primacy of divine justice over security. This preference is manifested in a famous saying that sovereignty may sustain with disbelief, but not with injustice.

We may agree that not only for a Shiʿa thinker but also for anyone living in the 21st century, the preoccupation with certain societies or political parties regarding the equation of power, security and justice is not a novel aspiration. These concerns have reflections in many contemporary discussions on democratic systems. For instance, if a researcher delves into the depths of ideological conflicts between Republican and Democratic parties in the United States, they will realise that the main theoretical debate revolves around choosing between security and power on the one hand, and justice and freedom on the other as the most significant ethico-political debate in social life. By examining the teachings of Imam Hussein as a living moral role model engaged in one of the most tragic historical confrontations, this book also addresses many significant ethical equations of war and peace that can provide a lens to evaluate present-day conflicts and tragedies.

Let's keep in mind that the Islamic world is living in an era that carries vivid and distressing memories of the widespread violence perpetrated by groups such as the so-called ISIS, the Taliban, Boko Haram, and the UK/US/NATO/Israeli-backed invasions of Palestine, Iran, Iraq, Syria, Yemen, Libya, Sudan, Lebanon, as well as the Indian State oppression in Kashmir. With the help of analyses that we have in this book, and based on the teachings of the tragedy of Karbala experienced by Imam Hussein and his companions, the Muslim world could successfully establish a non-violent political philosophy to not only construct a certain unified way of thinking but also shape the tangible socio-political life for the present and future generations all over the globe. If that could happen, then it would be safe to say that this book achieved its goal.

I would like to express my gratitude and deep appreciation to Professor Fanaie for this enlightening special edition. Its novel academic and analytical approach establishes an excellent scholarship in contemporary Imam Hussein Studies which I would regard as useful for seminarian as well as university curricula.

Mohammad Jafar Amir Mahallati
Professor of Religion, Oberlin College, Ohio, USA

Then, O sleepers, mourn for yourselves
For this heavy slumber is an evil death

Rumi

This book is a moral explanation of the Battle of Karbala. The event is multidimensional and warrants reflection and analysis from various perspectives, many of which have indeed been presented before. Historians and analysts who have studied the event have somewhat highlighted the moral subtleties, considerations, values and virtues evident in the character and actions of Imam Hussein, his family and companions. That being said, it would seem that the existing literature on the Battle of Karbala has not offered a *comprehensive* moral explanation of Imam Hussein's stance; hence, there is a need to articulate the moral principles governing his actions and reactions, and the virtues shaping his personality as the central figure of this highly significant event. This book attempts to take a small step towards filling this gap.

The explanation of historical events is subject to errors and oversights that analysts should strive to avoid; perhaps the most important of these being the fallacy of anachronism. Simply put, anachronism is the attribution of new concepts, or new definitions of old concepts, to individuals or groups who lived in the distant past. The literature of modern and contemporary ethics encompasses important distinctions, such as between religion and morality; the public sphere and the private; social/public and personal/

private morality; political and comprehensive conceptions of justice; rightness and goodness; church and state; ethical and meta-ethical theories; and topics such as human rights and citizenship. These have emerged as a result of gradual advances in ethics, and do not seem to have had a strong presence in the mentality and culture of people who lived in the pre-modern world.

Moreover, we are facing the inevitable and irreconcilable multiplicity of comprehensive moral, religious and philosophical systems in large and advanced modern societies – a situation perhaps less occurrent in pre-modern societies.

It seems, at first glance, that we have two options in such a predicament: either give in to the fallacy of anachronism or give up trying to learn from history by studying and appreciating it. Is there a third option? My answer to this question is the affirmative, for the following reasons:

First, fundamental moral principles and virtues have been present in human culture since ancient times. These include justice, courage, generosity, humility, forgiveness, human dignity, and both inner and outer freedom. The same is true regarding metaethical theories about the nature of moral goodness and badness and their relation to divine command and the edicts of rulers; the precedence of justice over political authority or vice versa; and awareness of the diversity of human motivations in moral behavior, among others.

Second, the attribution of new concepts or new definitions of old concepts to the past – the fallacy of anachronism – is one thing; answering the question of what historical figures, such as Imam Hussein, would say and do in the face of the issues, problems and questions we deal with in our context and time, is another thing altogether.

Therefore, in my opinion this question can be answered without falling into anachronism. However, in order to do so, one must implement thought experiments, undergo cultural translation, distinguish between what is essential and what is accidental, and stage a rational reconstruction of what has been done or said in the past. This is the method that I have employed in the moral explanation of the Battle of Karbala, although it is up to the readers to judge my success in this regard. In my approach, I have simply tried to answer the question of what Imam Hussein would say and do if he lived in our context by studying, analysing, and expounding what he said and did in his own context of yore.

This book contains three interviews and three articles organized into five chapters. The first interview (Chapter One) entitled, "Karbala: The Scene of the Confrontation Between 'Alawīte Islam and Umayyad Islam", endeavours to place the Battle of Karbala in its historical context; introduce Imam Hussein as a moral and spiritual role-model for humanity; as well as explore and explain the logical ramifications and implications of this view. This interview was conducted on 24 August 2020 at the House of Humanities Thinkers in Tehran. I sincerely thank all the management and staff of the House of Humanities Thinkers, especially Dr Mohammad Jalali and Mr Mehdi Simaei, the host of the programme, for the invitation and for making the necessary arrangements for recording and broadcasting the interview online.

The second and third interviews (Chapter Two) entitled, "The Battle of Karbala from a Moral Perspective", show that a moral explanation of the battle of Karbala is not only possible, but also desirable. In the course of these two interviews, three important moral principles are emphasised as a basis for explaining the important decisions that were made by Imam Hussein: the Principle of Justice, the Principle of Human Dignity and the Principle of Freedom. The role of the common approaches and theories of normative ethics in explaining the Battle of Karbala is also explored in these interviews. The last topic addressed in these interviews is the Ethics of Mourning.

These two interviews were held at Kashan's Imam Hussein Cultural Centre in the form of a series of online conversations entitled, "Condoling with the Sun" on 23/9/2020, transcribed by Abdul-Rasoul Kohanzad from the Majd Research Centre in Shiraz, and reviewed and rewritten by myself. I sincerely thank all the management and staff of the Imam Hussein Cultural Centre for the invitation and for making the necessary arrangements for recording and broadcasting the interviews online. I would also like to thank my colleague, Dr Hamed Shivapoor, who took on the responsibility of organising the meeting and designing the questions.

The first article in this collection (Chapter Three) entitled, "Common Explanations of the Battle of Karbala", attempts to review, analyse, and critique some of the most important and common explanations of this event; namely, mythical or metaphysical, political, and jurisprudential. The first edition of this article was presented in a public lecture on 1/5/2008 at the Tawhid Centre in London.

The second article in this collection (Chapter Four), entitled, "Hussein: The School of Justice and Dignity", explains the importance and status of justice and dignity among moral values; delineates the mechanisms, conditions and stages of the realisation of social justice; and attempts to explain the journey of Imam Hussein from Medina to Mecca and then Karbala in light of the principle of justice and the principle of dignity. The first edition of this article was presented as a public lecture on 8/8/2008 at Tawhid Centre in London. I sincerely thank Mr Mohammad Reza Jalaeipour for his invitation and for arranging the presentation of these two articles.

The third article in this collection (Chapter Five), entitled, "Religious and Meta-Religious Morality in Karbala", explains one of Imam Hussein's sayings in Karbala and elucidates the relationship between religious and meta-religious ethics. These two moral systems differ from each other more in the domains of moral psychology and the motivational reasons for action than in their value and normative content. The first edition of this article was read in a public lecture held on Ashura on 16/11/2013 to a group of students and Iranian compatriots residing in Cambridge. I would like to express my gratitude to the organisers for the invitation to this event.

I would also like to thank Dr Seyyed Rasoul Mousavi and Dr Mohammad Hussein Motahhari for assisting me in sourcing most of the sources and documents used in these interviews and articles and compiling the list of references. Dr Seyyed Amir Hussein Husseini and Seyyed Emad Tabatabai have added to the richness of the discussion in the first and second articles of this collection with their written and spoken criticisms and suggestions. A long, challenging and enlightening conversation with Dr. Mohammad Amir Quddusi prompted me to add an explanation of my method and some of my premises in the moral explanation of the Battle of Karbala in this introduction.

Finally, I would like to express my heartfelt gratitude to Dr Mohammad Jafar Mahallati and his colleagues at the Majd Research Centre in Shiraz, as well as to Mr Akbar Ghanbari, manager of Negāh-e Moʻāṣer Publications. I am also deeply indebted to the distinguished translator of this book, Dr El-ham Farahani and to the respected editor, Dr Hassan Shikoh. May Allah Almighty bless all these esteemed individuals with continued health and ever-growing success.

Abolghasem Fanaei
April 2025

Karbala: The Scene of the Confrontation between ʿAlawīte Islam and Umayyad Islam

Simaei: We are honoured to be with you in the second night of Muḥarram in the House of Humanities Thinkers. Tonight, we have Dr Fanaei from Qom as our guest. What is special about this year's programme is that all our guests will focus on the ethical aspects of the Battle of Karbala. Indeed, no one can deny or hesitate to accept the political significance of this movement. If one limits this event to only one aspect, they have actually falsified it. But proving an aspect does not negate the others, and a precise and all-encompassing look at this event would be one that includes all the aspects and considers all the viewpoints to get a more accurate perception – one which is more appropriate in comparison with others.

In tonight's programme, Dr Fanaei will focus on this topic and the differences between ʿAlawīte Islam and Umayyad Islam. As you may know, the first dispute in Islam is not the Shiʿa and Sunni dispute, or even that of two sects of one religion or a theological discord, but it was a political dispute which led to an ongoing clash between two radically different conceptions of Islam: i.e., ʿAlawīte Islam and Umayyad Islam. The literature on this topic is rich. As a prime example, the book Reflection of Ottoman Thought in Karbala[1] deals with it well. There is also some other research on the ʿAlawīte and Ottoman conflict. This is totally different from the Shiʿa and Sunni Islam which resulted from the construction of

---

[1]   Hedāyatpanāh (2009/1388).

7

theological and jurisprudential branches. The Ottomans developed through the Umayyad era. Later, in Imam Ṣadiq and Imam Baqir's era, the construction of the Shi'a happened. I will stop here and begin my conversation with Dr Fanaie. Dr Fanaie, the floor is yours now.

Fanaei: In the name of God, the Compassionate the Merciful. Hello, everyone. I thank my friends in the House of Humanities Thinkers who gave me another opportunity to share my moral explanation of the battle of Karbala and the lessons we can learn from it. The title of my speech is "Karbala: the Scene of the Confrontation Between 'Alawīte Islam and Umayyad Islam". Before going to the main point, I need to elaborate on some of the preliminary aspects of my discussion.

1.1. Various Aspects of the Battle of Karbala

Let me start my discussion by focusing on the important point that you just referred to in your opening remarks. The point is that the Battle of Karbala has various dimensions, and those who attempted to explain it have done so in accordance with the external conditions in which they lived and their own background. They have tried to look at it from a particular perspective, naturally highlighting some of its aspects and neglecting or downplaying others. In my opinion, one very important dimension that has been overlooked in explaining and describing the event is its moral and spiritual aspect.

I have tried to look at this issue from this angle, and as you said, it does not contradict that this event has other dimensions which can be viewed from various perspectives.

1.2. What Should We Expect from Imam Hussein?

The initial question we need to consider is, "What do we want from Imam Hussein and what are our expectations of him?" In my perspective, this is a crucial starting point. It is important for us to be mindful of our intentions when approaching Imam Hussein. What specific problems, concerns, or needs do we believe he can assist us with? Those who turn to figures like the Imam often have distinct challenges, questions, needs and concerns. They believe that by familiarising themselves with him and establishing a connection, they can find answers and attain satisfaction for their particular needs and concerns. The reason/s behind one's individual approach to Imam Hussein is indeed the focal point of my inquiry. However, it is essential to clarify that the initial question should be, "What should be our personal reason for turning to Imam Hussein?" rather than considering the reasons of others. This distinction highlights that our inquiry is "normative", not "descriptive". The aim is to evaluate and rectify our own justification and motivation in building a relationship with the Imam.

I think the most appropriate reason is to consider Imam Hussein as a role model. The Imam is someone who can and deserves to be a role model and exemplar for us. This is at least an important part of the meaning of Imamate in Shiʻa culture. In life and death, we need a role model; and our way of living and dying is influenced by the exemplar we have

9

chosen for this purpose. Imam Hussein's life and death make him a remarkable role model who can inspire all human beings from diverse backgrounds, different branches of Islam, and various other ideologies. His life and death resonate as a consistent source of inspiration, capable of influencing our decisions and actions throughout our life and even in the face of death.

Here, the multifaceted characteristics of Prophet Muhammad demand our attention, particularly his role as a prophet and an apostle. It is important to recognise the significance of both prophecy and apostlehood and understand their relationship. While many may consider the two to be interchangeable, there is a distinction between them. Apostlehood encompasses prophecy; that is, prophecy is a specific type of apostlehood. Among the diverse apostolic roles of the Prophet, prophecy held a prominent position. However, his prophetic role concluded with the end of prophecy, indicating that there will be no more prophet or messenger after him. Nevertheless, his other roles and missions continue without interruption until the end of the world. According to the Shi'a perspective, these roles are initially entrusted to the Imams and then extend to all Muslims, and even humanity as a whole. In my opinion, based on the inference from verse 33:21 of the Qur'ān, one of the most important missions that Prophet Muhammad had was to present himself as a successful, tangible and ideal role model for humanity, so that his audience would not deal with his ideas and teachings in merely theoretical, abstract or mechanical ways.

In Islamic culture, there is a common interpretation that distinguishes between two types of Qur'ān: the silent and the speaking. Prophet Muhammad should be considered to be the first speaking Qur'ān as he embodies the teachings of the same in human form. In other words, if the Qur'ān were personified, it would be the Prophet himself. To effectively invite people to embrace Islam, it is insufficient to rely solely on a book like the silent Qur'ān. It is also necessary for individual/s to live according to these teachings and serve as embodiments of the same. By observing how these individuals react to various situations in everyday life and make decisions based on their knowledge of the Qur'ān, people can witness the practical application of Islamic principles. These individuals are often referred to as the "speaking Qur'ān" in religious literature (Ṣadr ad-Din Shirazi, 2004: 2/513Y Ḥurr al-Āmili, 1988: 27/34; Rayshahri et al., 2006: 4/534).

Asserting that the Prophet serves as proof of God to people goes beyond his role as a prophet delivering Divine messages. It also signifies that he himself is the speaking Qur'ān, and his very existence, life and death serve as evidence unto themselves. He is a role model for humanity. In my opinion, the family of the Prophet (Ahl al-Bayt) are the successors who carry on his legacy as role models for others. They bear the responsibility of being exemplary figures, just as the Prophet did. Imam Hussein, in one of his speeches, explicitly referred to himself as a role model (Abu Mikḥnaf, 1996: 172).[2]

[2] This title has also been pointed out in narrations with similar expressions. See, for example, al-Sayyid al-Radi, 1993: Sermon 125; al-Majlisi, 1982: 23/197-198, H. 29; 24/198, H. 25.

Simaei: This point completely contradicts some of the interpretations of the event of Karbala.

Fanaei: Yes, exactly. Interpretations that are not plausible are those that consider jihad and martyrdom as a personal and exclusive duty of the Imam, and say that the Imam's uprising was an act of devotional obedience, and that his uprising was based on a divine order addressed to him personally which cannot be generalised to others, to get killed, or interpretations that attribute the event of Karbala to the Imam's exclusive knowledge of the unseen which is not accessible to others. The preliminary points that I am going to present here operate like criteria based on which we can choose the best interpretation among the various available about the Battle of Karbala.

The first criterion for the validity of any explanation of this event is that it should not contradict the belief that the Imam is a role model. If an explanation contradicts this criterion, then it will contradict the mission of Imamate itself, and which would make at least the Shi'a belief effectively flawed.

Based on our narrations, "A Shi'a is a person who follows the steps of Ali" (Majlisi, 1982: 8/363), meaning that Ali is a role model for him/her. The same applies to Imam Hussein: a true follower of Imam Hussein is someone who lives and dies like Imam Hussein. Shortly, I will explain what characteristics this role model possesses, or should possess, in order for us to emulate.

In short, that Imam Hussein is a role model is a prerequisite for the credibility of any explanation of this event. Therefore, if an explanation from the beginning is inconsistent with this prerequisite, it should be set aside in favour of other explanations that fulfil this condition.

1.3. Who Can Choose Imam Hussein as a Role Model?

The second preliminary point of my discussion raises the following question: "Who can consider Imam Hussein as a role model?" Let's explore the different possibilities. The most common answer would be that "Imam Hussein is a role model for Shi'a Muslims." Another perspective would suggest that "Imam Hussein is a role model for all Muslims." However, there is a third possibility that asserts: "Imam Hussein is a role model for all human beings, irrespective of their religion, faith, nationality, sex, race, language, culture, or any other distinguishing characteristic."

In my opinion, the third possibility is accurate. One of the reasons for favouring this possibility is that the Qur'ān describes the Prophet as a "mercy to all creatures" (Qur'ān, 21:107), by extension indicating that the Shi'a Imams are also meant to be epitomes of mercy towards all humanity. If they are to be merciful to the world, they should possess the ability and potential to be chosen, or accepted, as role models by people from different backgrounds, beliefs, and customs. In light of this, I would say that confining Imam Hussein as a role model to a specific religion or creed is unjust to both the Imam and mankind.

1.4. Necessary Conditions of a Role Model

The third preliminary aspect of my discussion is that if someone wants to be a role model for others, they must possess qualities that can be generalised to others; and if they aspire to be a role model for all humanity, their foundational qualities must be applicable to all humans. This means that the role model should live, decide and act based on values and norms that can encompass all individuals, regardless of their differences. They should be the subject and recipient of those values and norms, and all humans should have cognitive access to them. Furthermore, those values and norms should be able to generate in all humans the necessary motivation for living and acting in accordance to them.

In the upcoming chapters , I will delve into the concept that these universal values and norms can be understood as meta-religious morality. As said before, if the values and norms followed by Imam Hussein were solely based on Shi'a jurisprudence, limited to the Shi'a sect, then he cannot be considered a role model for individuals outside of Shi'a Islam. Similarly, if the foundational values and norms that shaped his decisions and actions are exclusive to Islamic jurisprudence, Imam Hussein's ability to inspire non-Muslims as a role model diminishes. Consequently, explanations that seek to interpret Imam Hussein's uprising solely through the lens of Shi'a or Islamic jurisprudence lose credibility, as they fail to align with his status as a universal role model for humanity.

1.5. What is Essential and Accidental in a Role Model?

The fourth preliminary aspect of my discussion can be presented in the form of the following question: "In what aspect(s) is Imam Hussein a role model?" This question holds significance as Imam Hussein possesses a multifaceted and multidimensional personality. Just like Prophet Muhammad is not merely a prophet, Imam Hussein transcends the confines of being solely an imam. However, it is essential to acknowledge that Imam Hussein, along with other historical and contemporary figures, cannot be universal role models in *every* aspect of our lives. For instance, Imam Hussein's activities such as traveling on horseback, engaging in combats with spears and swords, using firewood for warmth and cooking, and relying on olive oil for lighting are not areas where we seek him as a role model, let alone needing one.

To address this question, we encounter a significant dichotomy known as what is *essential* versus what is *accidental*. Although these two notions are applicable to various domains and subjects, they hold particular relevance when considering role models. The aim is to identify the fundamental aspects of role models while disregarding their accidental traits. Role models are not defined by their accidental attributes, but rather by their essential characteristics. In the following examples, I will elaborate on this assertion.

Imam Hussein was a man, but does his gender restrict him from serving as a role model for women too? Also, the language he spoke was Arabic. Should this imply that we must exclusively speak Arabic or that he is solely a role model for Arabic speakers? Likewise, Imam Hussein donned traditional Arabic attire, but should this automatically elevate Arabic clothing to the pinnacle of ideal attire?

~∞~

Simaei: I think you want to go even further and say that all spatiotemporal elements are accidental. To truly make Imam Hussein a role model for all, we should focus on the aspects of his personality that transcend time and place. While he lived in a specific context with its own unique elements, not all of those elements can be universally applied. Therefore, we should extract the essential qualities from his life that have broader relevance.

Imam Hussein's actions and interactions within the Umayyad Islamic era hold both contextual and transcendent aspects. The contextual aspects are tied to the specific time and place in which he lived, and they may not directly apply to us in our different circumstances. However, there are also meta-spatiotemporal aspects that can be extracted and applied to any setting. By identifying and focusing on these meta-spatiotemporal aspects of Imam Hussein's personality, we can find guidance that is relevant to us regardless of our own spatiotemporal contexts. These essential qualities offer us timeless principles and values that we can adopt as guidance for our own lives.

Do you apply the same principle of removing the elements of time and place to other figures like Prophet Muhammad, other Imams, Sharī'a rules, or the entirety of the religion? While this question may divert our attention from the main discussion, it is worth considering whether we should universally adopt Imam Hussein as a role model by eliminating spatiotemporal factors. If the answer is in the affirmative, then the same reason would dictate that all Imams and the Sharī'a rules established in various contexts should also be subject to this approach.

Fanaei: This question holds significant importance. However, before I address it, allow me to rectify an oversight in your statement. You are right in saying that accidentals encompass aspects that are unattainable in the new context due to our limitations or lack of resources and power; however, they also include achievable aspects which could be regarded as imprudent or nonsensical. For instance, while it is still possible to travel using horses and camels rather than cars, trains and airplanes, or engage in warfare with spears and swords instead of cannons, tanks, airplanes and missiles, such choices are irrational in our age.

Furthermore, the distinction between the essential and the accidental does not necessarily entail disregarding accidentals altogether. In some cases, it involves embracing a "cultural translation" of the same. Take, for instance, when we proclaim Imam Hussein as our inspirational figure in both war and peace: It means that we adopt his values and principles as the foundation for our decisions regarding warfare and peaceful situations, rather than replicating the specific weaponry he employed, such as spears, swords, bows and arrows. We look up to him for guidance on abstaining from gruesome acts like impaling the heads of our enemies on spears, mistreating prisoners, denying access to water, engaging in war without first exploring peaceful negotiations, initiating unprovoked attacks, and so forth. In essence, it is both meaningful and necessary to differentiate between the essential and accidental aspects within the entire realm of religion. For example, language is considered an accidental element as it represents a particular means of communication. In the context of Islam, Arabic is one of these accidental features. Furthermore, the cultural practices that prevailed during the time of the Qur'ān's revelation and the recording of historical accounts also fall into this category of accidentals, as do certain other prevalent discourses of that era.

The assertion that religious texts and religion itself comprise essentials and accidentals can be further clarified through reflection and the provision of concrete examples. This distinction does not require elaborate explanations or supporting arguments since it is widely accepted by numerous scholars and traditional jurists. However, it is important to note that any discrepancies that may arise lie in the delineation, limits, boundaries and scope of this distinction.

Let's examine a straightforward example in theology: Throughout the Qur'ān, the male pronoun is consistently employed to refer to God. However, it is important to note that this linguistic practice does not imply that the God of Islam is inherently male in terms of gender and identity. Rather, it reflects a feature of the Arabic language and culture that has become associated with Islam. Had the Qur'ān been revealed in a different language like Persian, for instance, such linguistic restrictions would not have been imposed on the speaker; instead there would then have been other Persian-language contexts for the revealed verses/revelation.

Once we acknowledge the presence of both essentials and accidentals within religion, such as religious texts and role models, and recognise the importance of differentiating between them in the realms of religious knowledge and practice, we are confronted with a series of significant questions that demand a lucid and definitive response. These would entail the following questions:

1. What criteria should be employed to differentiate between the essential and the accidental?
2. To what extent does this distinction extend, and what does it encompass?
3. Are essentials and accidentals static, or can they undergo transformation? In other words, is it conceivable for something that was once considered essential to become accidental at a later stage, and vice versa?
4. Do essentials and accidentals possess varying degrees of importance, or do all essentials hold equal weight?

These questions hold great significance. While we may not have definitive answers to them presently, it is crucial to acknowledge the distinction between essentials and accidentals in theology, jurisprudence and the interpretation of religious texts. Both sides of the argument require equal caution since treating accidentals as essentials or vice versa would be considered heretical and contrary to religious commitment. It is irrational to assume that a certain teaching should be deemed essential or accidental in cases of doubt without sufficient evidence.

In the realm of religious teachings and texts, we encounter a combination of essential and non-essential elements. This give rise to questions such as, "Is this particular teaching fundamental or incidental?" or "Does this specific Qur'ānic verse or historical account convey essential principles or non-essential details?" These questions can be applied to every teaching within the system and every sentence in religious texts. While some answers may be readily apparent, others may require further exploration. For instance, within Islam, certain aspects like monotheism, resurrection and the prophecy of Prophet Muhammad are considered essential tenets. On the other hand, while the obligation of paying *zakat* is an essential principle, determining which assets are subject to it falls under accidental considerations.

The following point may seem digressive, but it is crucial to highlight it: It is possible for a teaching to be accidental but not historical. Being accidental implies dependence on context, yet this dependency on context differs from reliance on history or confinement to a specific historical period. Put simply, historical context is merely a subset of overall context. For instance, presently there are regions on Earth devoid of electricity, gas, oil, cars, trains or airplanes. In these areas, residents likely employ tools and equipment for travel and the generation of heat and light that were used during pre-Islamic or early-Islamic periods. Consequently, if religious texts permit the use of impure olive oil in oil-burning lamps, this Sharī'a rule could remain valid and applicable within that particular region of the planet. Hence, when we assert that a religious teaching is accidental, it implies that it is specific to a particular context. However, whether that context is historical and confined to the past, incapable of re-emerging or being realised in the present or future, remains a separate question.

For instance, Islam mandates the performance of *wuḍu* for prayer and permits *tayammum* as an alternative when water is unavailable. Consider a scenario where, due to climate change, water becomes scarce for a continuous span of one thousand years. During this period, we would resort to *tayammum* for prayer. However, if after one thousand years the climate eventually changes and grants us abundant water for *wuḍu*, we cannot simply deem the requirement of *wuḍu* as being heretofore obsolete or expired. Consequently, accidental aspects themselves can be categorised into various types. Some of these are inherently unrelated to religion since their inception, while others are intricately linked to religion and subject to certain conditions and contexts. Regardless of the extension of a religious teaching to all times and places, applying it to our present circumstances relies on demonstrating that the context in which we currently live bears similarities in the relevant aspects to the context in which the Qur'ānic verse or hadith containing that religious teaching was revealed or issued.

Simaei: Indeed, while the examples provided shed light on the matter, there is a crucial aspect of the concept that requires further explanation. It is widely acknowledged that certain Sharī'a rules undergo changes over time. However, extending the differentiation between the essential and the accidental to encompass the entirety of religion goes beyond simply comparing the influence of time and place on Sharīʿa rules and the role of time and place in *ijtihad* (interpretation of religious law). If feasible, allow me to elaborate on the fundamental concepts of essentials and accidentals. Moreover, I would like to mention that Soroush (2008) takes it a step further by asserting that jurisprudence as a whole is an accidental aspect of religion.

Fanaei: If by "jurisprudence" Soroush means the field of legal scholarship, then it can be said that it is accidental. However, if by "jurisprudence" he means Sharīʿa, encompassing religious obligations and prohibitions, I find it difficult to agree with that assertion. From my perspective, Sharīʿa itself comprises two distinct categories of rules: essential rules and incidental rules.

Simaei: Are you referring to broad concepts such as the importance of gratitude, the value of justice, and the harm caused by injustice? Or are you suggesting that there may be additional elements beyond these fundamental principles?

Fanaei: These are moral rules. I'm referring to rules such as the prohibition of associating partners with God (*shirk*) and the prohibition of oppression, which are among the fundamental principles of Islam. Additionally, there are rules related to the objectives of Sharīʿa, such as the obligation to protect life, property, wealth, and reputation. Many jurisprudential rules, such as the prohibition of causing harm (*ḍarar*) and the prohibition of hardship (*mashaqqah*), fall under this category. Furthermore, there are general obligations, including performing *ṣalah* (prayer), observing fasting, performing *Ḥajj* (pilgrimage) and giving *zakat* (charity). These rules form the core structure of Sharīʿa.

It is important to note that while some of these rules may originate from moral considerations, such as the importance of justice and the evil of injustice, Sharīʿa rules differ from purely moral rules. They encompass a broader scope and have specific religious significance and application.

For instance, Prophet Muhammad's statement, "In Islam, there shall be no harm inflicted or reciprocated" (al-Ḥur al-ʿAmili, 1988: 26/14) emphasises that regardless of any changes or developments within Islamic Sharīʿa, the principle of avoiding harm will always remain unchanged. Similarly, when he referred to Islamic Sharīʿa as "easy" and "undemanding" (Koleyni, 1986: 5/494), he meant that this characteristic would endure even amidst changes in the Islamic legal framework.

Likewise, when we have narrations with themes such as, "Do not abandon prayer in any situation" (al-Ḥur al-ʿAmili, 1988: 4/241) or "Do not leave prayer in any situation, for the Prophet said: 'Prayer is the pillar of your religion'" (al-Ḥur al-ʿAmili, 1988: 2/373), it means that prayer is essential to Islamic law or religion. However, the direction faced during prayer (*Qibla*), whether it be towards Jerusalem or Mecca;

or the method of purification for prayer (wuḍū and *tayam-mum*), are considered as accidental aspects.

Similarly, in the Qur'ānic verse, "And those in whose wealth is a recognised right for the beggar and the deprived" (51:19), and in Imam 'Ali's statement in *Nahj al-Balāghah* (Raḍhi, 1993: saying 330) regarding the obligation of the rich to provide for the needs of the destitute, we can understand that paying *zakat* (obligatory charity) to support the needy is an essential aspect of Sharī'a. However, the specific amount or percentage of *zakat*, its subjects and the methods of collection and distribution are considered accidental details that may vary based on different circumstances.

Simaei: It's great that you're delving into the realm of devotion and obedience, which raises a thought-provoking question: Are religious rituals inherently necessary or merely accidental?

Fanaei: The distinction between essentials and accidentals is pervasive; it encompasses rituals, customs, recommended acts (*mustaḥabbāt*), discouraged acts (*makrūhāt*), transactions, acts of worship, and even beliefs. For instance, the core Islamic principle affirming the existence of an afterlife, heaven, and hell stands as an essential tenet. However, specific details like the presence of trees, the existence of a sun, or the language spoken by the inhabitants in heaven fall into the realm of accidentals. These aspects may vary from person to person and are subject to change.

To clarify, when we proclaim Imam Hussein as a role model for all people, we don't imply that he serves as an exemplar in every possible aspect, including accidentals. Instead, his role model status extends solely to essential aspects, along with those accidental aspects that mirror the contextual similarities between Imam Hussein and us.

1.6. Imam Hussein: A Model of Morality and Spirituality

The fifth preliminary aspect of our discussion, building upon the fourth, emphasises that if Imam Hussein is to serve as a role model for all individuals, it is within the realms of morality and spirituality where his influence can be regarded as universally relevant and inclusive. To establish this, we must demonstrate that his actions, reactions and choices are deeply rooted in universal moral and spiritual principles. This necessitates understanding how we should lead our lives and face death if we aspire to embody those very principles. By doing so, we can truly assert that Imam Hussein is our exemplar in both life and death, guiding us toward a meaningful existence.

1.7. How to Know and Follow a Role Model

Presenting the sixth preliminary aspect of our discussion, we address the question of how a moral and spiritual role model can effectively guide us and fulfil their proper role in our lives. Additionally, we delve into the concept of being a role model and explore its meaning. At this juncture, it is important to acknowledge that there exist two distinct methods on this matter. While proponents of the traditional understanding of religion may have concurred with previous points, their perspective diverges from ours at this juncture.

In the first method, which adheres to the traditional approach of embracing spiritual and moral role models, there is a notable distinction. The role model's character becomes somewhat detached from our direct experience, leaving us with only oral or written accounts of their sayings and actions. These reports then assume the role of substituting the actual presence of role models in our lives. Consequently, we are left with a compilation of reports that necessitate interpretation and extraction of guidelines to shape our own lives. Based on this method, it seems as though the prophets and imams' purpose and mission were solely limited to conveying the divine message through language, diminishing their status as active agents. Under this assumption, if we were to replace the prophets and imams with alternative mediators for delivering the divine message, the outcome would remain unchanged. As an illustration, according to this method, God could have chosen to transmit the Qur'ān in the form of a book or tablet rather than sending it through a prophet.

In this method, the prophet is perceived solely as a messenger and the imam as a preacher of rules, nothing more. In Islam, the primary sources of religious knowledge are the Qur'ān and the Sunnah, which encompass the sayings, deeds and interpretations of whom we consider to be the infallible. Within the traditional method, the authority of prophets and imams stems from the fact that their sayings, deeds and interpretations serve as the basis for deriving general rules that followers should adhere to. Consequently, religiosity is defined by putting into practice the conceptual/propositional knowledge acquired through this method. However, this understanding tends to overlook the broader aspects of the prophets' and imams' personalities, characters and specific missions. Essentially, in this view, the speaking Qur'ān transforms into a silent Qur'ān, or silent Sunnah replaces the speaking Qur'ān.

In the second method, however, which I believe to be the correct one, the reports of the role model's sayings, deeds and interpretations are not primarily seen as a source for deriving Sharīʿa rules. Instead, these reports serve as a means to comprehend and reconstruct the character of the role model. Subsequently, we strive to place ourselves in the role model's position within our circumstances, envisioning how they would have acted or reacted in a similar situations. By adopting this approach, those who follow the example of prophets or imams engage in a "thought experiment" rather than solely adhering to the literal meaning of words and their specific implications. The focus shifts towards understanding the underlying principles and embodying the essence of the role model's character, transcending mere textual interpretation.

In this perspective, a pertinent question arises: If we consider Imam ʿAli, for instance, who used to anonymously distribute bread and dates to aid the poor, the deprived and the orphans in his time, what actions would he take to assist them if he were alive today? Similarly, contemplating Imam Hussein's refusal to swear allegiance to Yazīd, his act of sharing water with his adversaries, and his acceptance of Ḥurr's repentance, prompts us to ponder how he would respond in similar circumstances in our era. Furthermore, when we reflect on Imam Ṣadiq's instruction to his servant to sell his annual reserve of wheat at a fair price during a famine in Madinah, followed by purchasing the necessary amount of wheat and barley for their daily needs like ordinary people, we are encouraged to contemplate how he would address a comparable situation if he lived in our times. By engaging in such contemplation, we seek to understand how these revered figures would apply their principles and values to contemporary challenges, allowing us to draw inspiration and guidance from their example.

In this perspective, the role model's personality are emphasised. Rather than replacing his personality, his sayings or actions serve as sources that allow us to reconstruct and culturally interpret his character. This character essentially represents the teachings of Islam. In addition to the verbal and written accounts of these teachings (that is, the silent Qur'ān and Sunnah), we also require their embodiment (known as the Speaking Qur'ān). This refers to a living and tangible example who can demonstrate through practical actions what we can become if we adhere to religious teachings. Relying solely on the silent Qur'ān and Sunnah is regarded as insufficient for guidance. What truly matters here is not just one's behaviour but also one's way of being.

Religious teachings cannot be effectively conveyed by simply transferring information to the minds of the audience, much like the teaching of mathematics. Furthermore, the purpose of religious teachings extends beyond mere control of external behaviour, making it inadequate to rely solely on written or oral forms of these teachings to fulfil the goals of religion. We require models to emulate, not only in terms of outward conduct but also in temperament, personality, attitude, emotions and other life concerns.

The individuals we choose as moral and spiritual role models possess virtues that are ingrained and institutionalised within us through establishing a living and existential connection with them, existing alongside them. Therefore, what holds central importance here is the "existential" bond between two individuals, rather than a purely "mental" connection. While their sayings and reports about their behaviour aid in reconstructing these role models in our minds, they can never substitute for the actual presence of these people in our lives.

Indeed, the richness, depth and complexity of moral and spiritual life cannot be adequately encapsulated in one or more general and abstract principles. Similarly, the significance of moral and spiritual role models and their impact on the lives of others is too immense and profound for us to simply substitute their living presence with their words and behaviour alone.

It is worth emphasising that, just as in the realm of normative ethics where moral deontology and utilitarianism cannot replace virtue and exemplarist ethics, the same is true with regard to the domain of religion and Sharīʿa. In other words, akin to the realm of ethics, deontological and consequentialist perspectives in jurisprudence cannot supplant virtue jurisprudence that is centred on role models.

1.8. Existential Relationship with a Role Model

The seventh preliminary aspect of my discussion is that adopting a role model involves establishing an existential relationship with them, encompassing both emotional and cognitive aspects. However, this relationship has been largely fragmented in the case of Imam Hussein, and to a lesser extent in the case of other imams. Among Shi'a ordinary followers, emphasis has primarily been placed on the emotional connection with these figures, while Shi'a Scholars have focused more on the cognitive aspect. Unfortunately, for the majority of people, the cognitive dimension of their existential relationship with the imams has been completely neglected, leading to the proliferation of superstitions and fabricated ḥadiths. It is crucial to recognise that moral and spiritual role models can only have a meaningful impact when both the emotional and cognitive aspects are given equal importance. Distortion within this context manifests in various forms.

Regrettably, in the case of Imam Hussein, these two aspects have become detached from each other, which I would say is a form of distortion that hampers our understanding of him as being a spiritual and moral role model. Additionally, other distortions have also emerged, further undermining our ability to truly embrace Imam Hussein's exemplary character. Collectively, these distortions have had a detrimental impact on our capacity to emulate him.

To illustrate this point, let's consider the concept of intercession (shafa'ah). What does intercession truly mean and how does it function? It should not be misconstrued as favouritism or a means to seek immediate absolution for committing acts of injustice towards oneself or society. Mere participation in mourning events for Imam Hussein and thus hoping for his intercession, cannot erase one's misdeeds or remove the consequences of one's actions without requiring any lasting changes in behaviour or lifestyle on the part of the mourner.

Intercession occurs when a person's personality undergoes a transformation through their connection with Imam Hussein and the establishment of an existential relationship with him. This profound and enduring change begins to eliminate the effects of their past mistakes and sins on their soul. Furthermore, for their oppression or mistreatment of others, expiation or redress is possible by way of compensation in different ways. The true meaning of intercession and repentance, as well as seeking forgiveness, lies in the removal of both internal and external traces of error and sin. This process is not based on contracts or credits but rather on the existential and developmental relationship between one's actions and their impact on one's inner and outer being. When someone intercedes for a sinner, they bring about a transformation in their character, thereby deserving pardon and forgiveness.

In my view, it is crucial to recognise that mourning is not an end in itself, but a means to an end. It does not hold centrality but serves as a method. Under oppressive regimes, mourning becomes the only available avenue for commemorating and preserving the memory of the martyrs of Karbala. It also creates a suitable environment for establishing an existential bond with exemplary figures, such as Imam Hussein and his companions. However, if mourning becomes the ultimate goal and takes centre stage, then simply shedding tears in itself and at any cost, even if done so in response to distortions of history and misrepresentation of the Imam's character, becomes valorised. This approach towards mourning and its purpose and philosophy has been a significant incentive for scholars and the layman alike to fabricate retellings of the story of Karbala.

Two primary methods may be employed in the endeavour to achieve the above: The first involves putting a heavy emphasis on the atrocities committed by Yazīd and his army, effectively focusing on the dark chapter in the history of Karbala. This perspective, as expressed by Motahhari, aims to emphasise the crimes perpetrated during that time. Another approach involves lowering the Imam's stature down to the audience's level in order to arouse sympathy. The effects of the over-emphasis on the crimes of Yazīd's army is that they tend to overshadow the actions and teachings of Imam Hussein, which ultimately marginalises his significance. Additionally, in some instances, the image projected of Imam Hussein is often that of an individual preoccupied with matters such as Qasim's wedding, rather than focusing on the tragic situation at hand that eventually led to his martyrdom.

Simaei: It used to only happen with Imam Hussein, but now some people are distorting the character of Imam 'Ali as well. They see that embezzlement is becoming rampant, and they cite that there was a lot of corruption and embezzlement during Imam 'Ali's time. The reason for this perversion seems to be their newfound way to make up for not having got close to Imam 'Ali as they believe they should have before Imam 'Ali.

Fanaei: Yes, unfortunately, such a distortion has happened and is happening more or less in the case of all our Imams. The result of this attitude is that those who were supposed to be role models for others and play a role in their moral and spiritual education, lose their proper function in human development. The void thus created is filled by people that institutionalise moral and spiritual degeneration in individuals as well as the society. One cannot participate in mourning ceremonies for Imam Hussein while simultaneously treat others as if their role model were Yazīd.

The point I wanted to emphasise is that any deed or saying that overshadows or undermines Imam Hussein's position as a role model is invalid, and any explanation of the events of Karbala that ignores Imam Hussein's place as a role model is incorrect and unacceptable. An emotional relationship with Imam Hussein is necessary, but it is insufficient, because such a relationship is valuable and effective only when it is accompanied by an accurate understanding and emulation of Imam Hussein's personality.

Therefore, the right way to mourn is that in which the personality of Imam Hussein is not distorted. Mourning means sympathising with Imam Hussein, seeing the world through his eyes, feeling what kind of situation and atmosphere he lived in and what kind of experience he went through. The philosophy of mourning is sharing in Imam Hussein's experience and undergoing a similar experience, however incomplete and diminished in form, in the realm of our imagination. Such a thought experiment is likely to help us live and die like Imam Hussein.

In any case, a real mourning ceremony for Imam Hussein is one in which upon the mourners' return to their daily life, the people around them and those who are in contact with them feel that they are not conscious deceivers, usurpers of people's rights, quarrelsome over worldly matters, or ruiners of others people's reputation for worldly gains.

1.9. The Confrontation between ʿAlawīte and Umayyad Islam in Karbala

Karbala is the scene of the confrontation between two interpretations of Islam. As you mentioned, these two readings have a long track record in Islamic history, and similar cases are found in other religions as well. We call these two readings, "ʿAlawīte Islam" and "Umayyad Islam". Both these have huge differences both in theory and practice, i.e., each of them has its own theoretical and practical theology. In my opinion, the most important difference between the two is in their views on the relationship between religion and morality: In ʿAlawīte Islam, it seems that morality comes before religion, while in Umayyad Islam, religion comes before morality.

These two readings of Islam have had and continue to have representatives, proponents, interpreters, commentators, spokespersons, role models and followers in every era. In Karbala, Yazīd and his army are the role models of Umayyad Islam, while Imam Hussein and his followers are the role models of 'Alawīte Islam. Thus, Karbala is the scene of the confrontation between these two types of role models. The two opposing parties made decisions and acted based on certain foundations and premises. As people who have chosen to take Imam Hussein as the ideal man, it is important for us to know the method and bases of his decision-making, actions and reactions as well as of those who were involved against him. This is because following a role model in action means knowing that role model's method and principles of decision-making and living according to those methods and principles.

In the decision-making process, two types of premises should be combined with each other to answer the question, "What should be done in this particular situation?" or "How should I act in this particular situation?". The first type are the premises that *describe* the existing situation, and the second type are the evaluative and normative premises that *prescribe* or *recommend* what should be done to realise the ideal situation. By combining these two types of premises, a person is able to come to a decision that they think might be in line with the Imam's had the Imam been in a similar situation. The difference between 'Alawīte Islam and Umayyad Islam in terms of decision-making mainly originates from their difference in the second type of premises, i.e., evaluative and normative.

Every decision we make is based on the knowledge we have of our current situation, and the soundness of any decision depends on the validity of the sources and ways and methods through which this knowledge was obtained. For example, in Karbala, in order to make a wise decision, Imam Hussein did not limit himself to the invitations he received from the people of Kufa, but he also consulted with the knowledgeable people of the time and sent Muslim ibn 'Aqīl to Kufa to investigate the situation up close and report back to him.

In the common explanations of the events of Karbala, Imam Hussein is depicted either as someone who received the necessary values and norms for making his decisions in the form of a private order from God, or as a committed Muslim who received these values and norms from the Islamic Sharī'a, as if meta-religious ethical considerations did not play any role in his decision-making.

I believe that neither of the aforementioned is the case, and it can be shown that throughout his movement, he made decisions and acted based on universal moral principles or virtues which are not specific to Muslims or the Shi'a. In fact, as I said before, one of the most prominent differences between 'Alawīte Islam and Umayyad Islam goes back to this, i.e., the role that meta-religious morality plays in a believer's decisions. This is precisely what shows that Imam Hussein is a role model for all of humanity, and not just for Muslims or the Shi'a.

We see many moral principles manifested in the deeds and sayings of Imam Hussein and his companions, but it seems that among these principles there are three that are more significant than the others. These are: (1) the principle of justice, (2) the principle of human dignity, and (3) the principle of freedom. The third principle of course has a vertical relationship with the other two and is not a horizontal one; it expresses the pure motivation for an ethical life and behaviour, which is the commitment to moral values for the sake of these values themselves and not for the fear of or greed to-

36

wards the consequences of one's behaviour. Imam Hussein's decision to fight oppression in the interests of the establishment of a just political system can be explained based on the first principle, and his decision to refuse to swear allegiance to Yazīd, accept humiliation or submit to his oppression can be explained based on the second principle.

CHAPTER TWO

The Battle of Karbala from a Moral Perspective

Shivapoor: Welcome to the *Ta'ziate Aftab* programme. As you may be aware, the Cultural Centre of Imam Hussein annually commemorates the ritual of Arba'een. However, this year, due to the ongoing Coronavirus-related lockdowns, we have adapted the programme into a virtual format. The central focus of our programme throughout the years has revolved around elucidating the significance of Imam Hussein's uprising, the narrative of Karbala, and the 'Ashura movement. Today, we are honoured to have with us Dr Fanaei, a distinguished scholar renowned for his extensive research on the interplay between religion and morality, particularly in relation to the uprising of Imam Hussein and the Ashura movement. He has authored several significant books and articles on these subjects. Following his introduction, I will proceed to ask him my questions. Welcome, Dr Fanaei.

Fanaei: Thank you. In the Name of God, the Compassionate, the Merciful. I extend my warm greetings to you and the esteemed audience of this programme. I would also like to express my sincere gratitude to our dear colleagues for their valuable time and efforts they have dedicated towards making this programme possible.

2.1. Multiple Explanations of the Battle of Karbala

Shivapoor: As you are aware, in recent decades, there have been numerous interpretations, explanations, and readings of the story of Karbala and the uprising of Imam Hussein. One of the earliest and most controversial interpretations in our country was proposed by Ṣāliḥī Najafābādī. His reading primarily focused on a political explanation according to which, Imam Hussein's intention for uprising was introduced as an endeavour to establish an Islamic government.

Similarly, Sharī'atī's works contained significant political elements too. However, he also presented a mythological interpretation in his work *Hussein, the Heir of Adam*. Another notable perspective is Moṭahhari's explanation which suggests that the objective of Imam Hussein's uprising was to promote "enjoining good and forbidding evil." Throughout the four decades following the Islamic revolution, various contemporary thinkers and writers have offered their own perspectives on this historical event.

Dr Fanaei, among these explanations, there seems to be a lack of emphasis on the ethical dimension. While it is possible for multiple aspects to coexist, it is rare to find interpretations that centre around morality. For instance, Ṣāliḥī Najafābādī's interpretation, which views the secret behind Imam Hussein's uprising as the establishment of an Islamic government, can also be considered a moral interpretation – that the formation of an Islamic government is a moral endeavour. However, such perspectives are scarce or non-existent, at least from what I have observed in the relevel literature.

Dr Fanaei, my first question is this: "Does the Battle of

Karbala have the potential to be interpreted in light of moral considerations?" If the answer is yes, I would like to know: "How and what moral values should be emphasised in this type of interpretation?"

2.2. The Moral Explanation of the Battle of Karbala

Fanaei: This is an important question that necessitates a detailed response. However, the short answer is yes. Before delving into the specifics, I would like to address two preliminary points. Firstly, the terminology we use, such as "uprising", reflects a particular perspective on the nature of Imam Hussein's actions. This attitude warrants further discussion, and for the sake of neutrality, I propose employing a more impartial term like "movement." Whether Imam Hussein's movement can be classified as an uprising, an act of defence, a reform, a revolution, or something else entirely remains debateable. When describing and explaining the events of Karbala, in principle, it is crucial to avoid anachronism and to refrain from attributing concepts from later periods in human culture to a specific historical period.

However, this historical event demands our attention for two significant reasons. Firstly, it holds immense importance due to its tragic and painful nature. Secondly, as individuals with religious and moral convictions, we seek to derive valuable lessons from it and incorporate those lessons into our lives. Consequently, its investigation and elucidation hold great significance for us in numerous ways.

For centuries, the prevailing interpretation of the event within Shi'a culture was rooted in mythology. According to this interpretation, it was believed that God had ordained the occurrence of this incident within its specific historical and geographical context, and that God had willed the martyrdom of Imam Hussein and the capture of the women and children of Ahl al-Bayt. While there were alternative explanations put forth by both Shi'a and Sunni thinkers, they did not hold the same level of significance as the dominant interpretation.

In the contemporary era, several attempts have been made to provide non-mythological explanations for the events of Karbala or revive marginal explanations. Notable figures such as Sharī'atī (1997), Ṣāliḥī Najafābādī (1970), and Moṭahhari (1998) have contributed to this discourse. Their aim has been to explain this event in a way that others can learn from it and the Imam's behaviour can be adopted by others. Each of these thinkers has approached the event from a unique perspective, resulting in a wide variety of explanations in the literature of Ashura studies.

It is important to note that offering a moral explanation for the Battle of Karbala does not imply disregarding other contributing causes and factors. Events are typically shaped by a combination of various elements. However, when explaining this particular event, the focus is on understanding the underlying principles that guided the decisions and actions of those involved. The values and norms upon which their choices were based play a more prominent role compared to other factors.

The moral explanation of the Battle of Karbala revolves around the premise that the actors and instigators of this event adhered to two distinct and opposing sets of morals: *'Alawīte morality* and *Umayyad morality*. Given the significant political dimensions of the event of Karbala, the political aspects of these two ethical frameworks naturally take centre stage. Therefore, it would be appropriate to discuss 'Alawīte political ethics and Umayyad political ethics rather than solely focusing on their broader ethical systems.

2.3. The Connection between the Battle of Karbala and the Previous Events

Another point to consider is that historical events do not happen in a vacuum. It is not like, for example, a person or a group suddenly decides to create an event overnight. Certain things should happen, and then gradually various factors and actors come together and create a new context and situation. In that new situation, some individuals conclude that they have to do something, for instance, whether to defend, revolt, bring about a revolution or create a movement. The other side also decides that they too must react. To provide a thorough and accurate explanation of the tragedy of Karbala, therefore, it is crucial to trace it back to the origins of Islam, particularly the events that transpired after the passing of the Holy Prophet and the subsequent controversies about his succession. Additionally, examining the cultural norms, customs, morals and values prevalent among the Arab tribes before the advent of Islam becomes equally important. By doing so, we can better understand how certain practices throughout Islamic history, such as what happened in the Battle of Karbala, can be seen as a resurgence of the same values observed during the

Jāhiliyyah period.

In this regard, it seems that giving a correct explanation of the Battle of Karbala depends on the separation of two different readings of Islam; we call one of these readings *ʿAlawīte Islam* and the other *Umayyad Islam*. These readings differ from each other in several ways, including their position on the relationship between religion and morality in general, and on the politics or political morality in particular. The difference between these two readings of Islam is much more than their similarity; in fact, their similarity is more verbal than semantic and/ or thematic. In other words, their difference is so great and fundamental that it is as if we are dealing with two different religions that are only similar in their names.

For example, the existence of God is accepted in both readings of Islam, but they disagree about the nature of God. The God that Umayyad Islam introduces is tyrannical and autocratic, and humans are his slaves. His will is such that it leaves no room for the free will of man. On the contrary, the God whom ʿAlawīte Islam introduces is just, and humans can freely choose to become his servants, not his slaves. His justice takes precedence over His will, and His will follows His justice, not vice versa. Therefore, Divine will is compatible with man's free will. Further, the Prophet that Umayyad Islam introduces has a power-seeking and autocratic personality. He is authoritarian, that is, someone whose personality and behaviour changes when in power; and like all people in power throughout history, the power will change his nature, character, speech and behaviour towards enemies and opponents. This is in contrast with what the 'Alawīte Islam tells us about the Prophet.

These two views of the nature of God and Prophet in theoretical theology led to two different views in practical and political theology. Umayyad political theology is *power-centred*. In Umayyad Islam, political power is the end which has intrinsic value, while all other things, including justice, have instrumental value. The will of the tyrannical caliph or sultan, who is supposedly the representative of the tyrannical God, is the source of all values and whatever he wills is just by definition.

However, 'Alawīte political theology is justice-centred. In 'Alawīte political theology, justice has intrinsic value, and is the origin of all values. Certainly, in this theology, political power also has value, but it is not intrinsic; instead, it is instrumental and conditional. In other words, power and government are validated by justice, not the other way around. In this view, political power is considered valuable only to the extent, or under the condition, of that by which justice can be established and rights can be fulfilled. In this reading of Islam, justice is a meta-religious or meta-Divine standard which is independent of the will of the rulers, and by which the behaviour of the rulers is measured. It is for this reason that the division of rulers into just rulers and unjust rulers becomes paramount. If justice is solely determined by the rulers' will, the notion of an unjust ruler loses its meaning and application altogether.

The moral explanation of the Battle of Karbala tells us

that Karbala was a confrontation between these two readings of Islam. In it, we see a vivid and tangible image of the
embodied patterns of both readings of Islam. In the moral
explanation, the question is, "Did Imam Hussein have a moral reason for his decisions and behaviour from the very beginning of his journey to the end?"; "Did he make decisions
and act based on moral principles or based on other kind(s)
of normative principles?"; and, "If he made decisions and
acted based on moral reasons, what were those reasons?"
These are the questions that the moral explanation of the
Battle of Karbala tries to answer.

On the other hand, we already know that the actions of
the Umayyad party were immoral, but we need to know what
justification they had for their immoral behaviour and how
they convinced themselves to commit such violent crimes.
This is where this discussion relates closely to the discussion
of the relationship between religion and morality, because
even if we assume that the real justification of those people
for committing the crimes was a non-religious one, for example, to serve their worldly interests, they had to provide a
religious justification to defend their actions and persuade
the mass of people of their behaviour towards Imam Hussein
and his companions.

2.5. Separation of Religion from Morality and the Religious Justification of Violence

My hypothesis, based on which I will advance the discussion,
is that many of the great tragedies in the history of Islam, and
possibly in other religions too, are actually the result of sepa-

rating religion from morality – putting religion in the place of morality or giving priority to literal interpretation of religious texts over moral considerations in the case of conflict. Wherever religion is separated from morality, similar tragedies are likely to occur. Of course, this is not limited to religious worldviews; non-religious belief systems also have a similar fate.

From this perspective, we can claim that Imam Hussein's goal was to restore morality to its rightful place in religious knowledge and practice in general, and in politics in particular. Perhaps the most important difference between the 'Alawīte and Umayyad readings of Islam lies in their position on the relationship between religion and morality, especially in the realm of politics. In the 'Alawīte interpretation of Islam, morality acts as the framework of religion, whereas the Umayyad perspective lacks such a framework. To clarify further, the Umayyad interpretation replaces morality with political power, transforming religion into a means by which the powerful justify even their immoral acts of authority.

There is substantial evidence to support this claim. I will mention some of it as examples. The words of Imam 'Ali in *Nahj al-Balāghah* clearly show that in his reading of Islam, "justice has intrinsic value and political power has instrumental value" (e.g., see Sermons 33 and 224), and that the end does not justify the means (e.g., see Sermons 69, 126, and 200). However, in the Umayyad reading, the right belongs to the one who has more power and overcomes others by force, gaining and maintaining power have intrinsic value, and the end justifies the means. These values and their opposites are evident in the wars, conflicts and political disputes witnessed since the beginning of Islam.

For example, in the Battle of Ṣiffin, Muʿawiya's army managed to take control of the banks of the Euphrates and denied Imam ʿAli's troops access to its waters. In contrast, when Imam ʿAli was able to wrest control of the river from Muʿawiya, he ordered his soldiers to allow the enemy soldiers access to it, apprising them that they too have a right to use the resource (Menqari, 1983: 160-162). Likewise then, in his first encounter with the al-Ḥurr ibn Yazīd al-Riyāḥī's regiment on the way to Karbala, Imam Hussein provided them and their horses with his water from his supplies (al-Mufid, 1992: 2/78); however, later on when Umar ibn Saʿd's battalions besieged the Imam, his companions and his family, he blocked their access to the Euphrates (Majlisi, 1982: 45/51). It can be construed from this behaviour of the Umayyads that it is premised on their belief in the principle that the end justifies the means.

Another example is the character Muslim ibn ʿAqīl demonstrated in Kufa, to the suggestion that he could hide behind the curtain in Hani ibn Urwa's house and assassinate ibn Ziyad when he was visiting Hani (Abu Mikhnaf, 1996: 113-114). If Muslim ibn ʿAqīl had accepted the suggestion and assassinated ibn Ziyad, there was a strong possibility that Kufa could have been liberated, and Imam Hussein would have reached the city without impediment. This could have changed the course of history. However, Muslim ibn ʿAqīl did not accept the proposal to execute ibn Ziyad, citing the Prophet: "Islam prohibits assassination" (Kulayni 1986: 7/375; Majlisi 1985: 16/450-451). These behaviours exhibit that according to ʿAlawīte Islam, there are things a practicing Muslim should never do, whatever the cost. In other words, the end does *not* justify the means. Thus, these are some of the principles of the meta-religious morality which are recognised in the ʿAlawīte reading of Islam as the framework of religion. The Umayyad reading of Islam, however, does not always seem to recognise these principles and tends to violate them in practice.

2.6. Moral Principles Governing the Decisions of Imam Hussein

Now, when we use this perspective on the Battle of Karbala, we observe the three ʿAlawīte moral principles mentioned earlier that played a prominent role in Imam Hussein's decisions, actions and words. These explain his movement from beginning to end which are based on these three principles: justice, dignity, and inner freedom. Of course, this does not mean that other moral values were absent in the behaviour and actions of the Imam and his companions. It simply means that the three principles listed were the foundations for the Imam's momentous decisions. In addition, it goes without saying that the Battle of Karbala has includes religious and political aspects. The moral explanation in question does not deny or ignore them. Rather, it shows the relationship between religion, morality and politics from Imam Hussein's point of view. In other words, this explanation shows the significance of morality in the ʿAlawīte reading of Islam, especially in its practical and political theology.

2.6.1. Justice in the Battle of Karbala

Since I have already discussed these principles in detail, I would refer the readers to the later chapters of this book.

Here, I will briefly state that Imam's departure from Medina and his movement to Mecca and then Kufa can be explained by considering the principle of justice. One of the pieces of evidence supporting this claim is the Imam's last will to his brother, Muḥammad ibn al- Ḥanafīyah, which he wrote before leaving Medina. In it, he states:

> I did not rise (*akhruj*) with a motive of selfishness, nor a feeling of euphoria, nor to practice cruelty, nor to corrupt. Rather, I have risen (*kharajtu*) with the intention of reforming my grandfather's nation. I want to enjoin people to do good and forbid them from doing wrong and follow the lead (*sīrah*) of my grandfather and father (Majlisi, 1982: 44/329).

The verbs "*akhroj*" and "*kharajtu*" can be interpreted as either "departing from a place and moving towards another place" or "rising against the established political system". In any case, the Imam states that his motive for traveling from Medina or uprising is not personal gain, or being cruel, or corrupting the society or creating chaos; rather, he aims to improve the state of Islamic community, that is, "to provide public benefit". He rises for the purpose of enjoining good and forbidding wrong and seeks to emulate the very path of his father and grandfather. "*Sīrah*" in this context means "political management", which was based on justice during the time of the Prophet and Imam 'Ali, but that after their deaths, it was not.

Imam Hussein meant that the Islamic society had been afflicted by corruption which needed to be eliminated. It were the subtle deviations from the 'Alawīte political theology and replacement with the Umayyad version that the Imam protested against. The important point to note here is that in ruling in the name of religion, the caliphate is not merely a political position. When the caliph's method of governance is unjust, the people's religion will also become distorted both in the private and public spheres. In a theocracy, people tend to follow the religion of their ruler, thus, political and economic corruption is also given a religious justification – effectively, this is a kind of heresy and religious deviance. Consequently, every corruption is done in the name of religion and then it is the original religion that is tarnished.

The transformation of the caliphate into an absolute monarchy stands as the ultimate malevolence, giving rise to various other evils. This change aligning with the political ideology of Yazīd, namely Umayyad Islam and Umayyad political theology, exacerbates the impact of this wickedness. Yazīd's recitation of the famous poem, "Hashim and [his successors just] played with the kingdom; no news came nor revelation descended" (Ṭabrisī, 1982: 2/307), shows that he saw power as a plaything. In other words, the greatest evil was putting a cruel and autocratic God in the place of a just God. A tyrannical God would provide the theoretical support for the rule of a tyrannical king (*sultan*) and would give it religious legitimacy. This stands as the epitome of evil, unparalleled in its magnitude and the progenitor of all subsequent malevolence. Imam Hussein wanted to overcome and eliminate this evil. Naturally, by removing this evil, many other evils that originated from this would also be decimated. I am not saying that there were no other evils, but that this was the most significant one that had to be dealt with first. I believe this is the correct interpretation of the Imam's words.

Therefore, the interpretations premised on accusations such as, "Yazīd was a dog lover and a gambler" as being the Imam's intention for his uprising, somewhat distort the essence of the Battle of Karbala as far as the Imam is concerned. Also, interpretations that say, "People had become corrupt, and the Imam wanted to enjoin them to do good and forbid them from doing wrong through taking power and establishing an Islamic government", cannot be defended. This is because the greatest vice that ought to be reformed was the government itself, i.e., the method of governance.

Justice in this case means *political* justice which has nothing to do with personal justice because it is the most fundamental virtue of political institutions, not persons. Just as individuals are divided into just and unjust on the basis of their behaviour towards themselves and others, political institutions can also be categorised as either just or unjust, based on how they are formed and how they impact society. However, the important point to note here is that in terms of personal morality, putting people who are considered judicious in charge of political institutions does not necessarily make the institutions just as well.

The principle of justice, and the duty to try to establish a just government, explain Imam Hussein's movement well but only to some extent; that is, until it became clear that people of Kufa had failed to keep their word and were not willing to cooperate with the Imam. This is because eliminating such deep corruption and establishing a just political system is not possible without sufficient public support. A large group of people must help and be willing to make sacrifices. Also, the Qur'ān says, "Indeed we sent our messengers with clear signs, and sent down with them the Book and the Balance that *people* may uphold justice..." (57:25 [italics added]). Therefore, if the people are unwilling to contribute towards changing their own condition, the burden is lifted from the Imam's shoulders, although his duty of preaching may remain. (For more explanation, see Chapter 4).

2.6.2. Human Dignity in the Battle of Karbala

When Imam Hussein learnt that people of Kufa had changed their opinion and were not willing to cooperate, he concluded that he no longer had to shoulder the responsibility they had invited him to undertake; that is, to rise and reform the political system in order to establish a just government. Therefore, his subsequent decisions can be explained not on the basis of the principle of justice, but on the principle of human dignity. It is at this point that we observe the Imam making the decision that martyrdom with honour and dignity is better than a life of humiliation as the principle of human dignity dictates: "Human life is valuable as long as it is with dignity". From a moral point of view, life is not always valuable under all conditions and at any cost, but only a certain type of life is valuable – one in which human dignity is respected and not violated. (For more explanation, see Chapter 4).

2.6.3. Inner Freedom in the Battle of Karbala

Another moral value that had a prominent role in this event and was evident in the behaviour and speech of the Imam and his companions is that of inner freedom.[3] Many of the Imam's actions can be explained by referring to this value, including his acceptance of al-Ḥurr ibn Yazīd al-Riyāḥī's repentance; providing his enemy with water; offering his companions to abandon their allegiance to him on the night of 'Ashura; and when he absolved those who owed money of their obligation towards him, and to go and pay off their debts first. (For more explanation, see Chapter 5).

Thus, I think the three moral principles I listed can very well explain the Battle of Karbala. From this perspective then, one can conclude that Imam Hussein is not only a role model for Shi'as, but for all of humanity. This is because all human beings, regardless of race, religion, sect, nationality, and gender, are included in and addressed by these three basic moral principles, and can accept them and live according to them without any "religious" strings attached. Imam Hussein paid a heavy price for keeping alive and immortalising these principles by demonstrating the significance of their value. In the Imam's view, and in fact in 'Alawīte Islam, following these principles have such divine value that the Imam is willing to sacrifice his life for them. Thus, the commemoration of Imam Hussein and the martyrs and prisoners of the Battle of Karbala, whether it be in the form of mourning rituals or others ways, should be aimed at revitalising these very principles and values.

---

[3] Inner freedom is different from outer freedom, in that the latter means being free from restrictions imposed on one's will by external powers, while the former means being free from the shackles of the *nafs al-ammara*: fear and greed.

2.7. Religious Morality and Meta-Religious Morality in the Battle of Karbala

Shivapoor: Thank you Dr Fanaei. Very clear and useful explanation. My next question is about those golden words of Imam Hussein in his last moments: when he saw that the enemy forces closed in his tents, he said, "If you do not believe in religion, then at least be free in your worldly affairs." You have already discussed it elsewhere. I think this quote is related to our discussion. Please tell us how you think these words are important, and what can be learned from them?

Fanaei: I have already discussed this topic in detail, which is documented in an article. (See Chapter 5). It may not be feasible to delve into the entirety of this statement within our limited time, but I will briefly share some points here.

What the Imam meant was that their actions, that is, attacking the tents, setting fire to them and looting them, were wrong for two reasons: one, religious, and the other, moral or meta-religious. The religious reason can be effective and can prevent the individuals from committing the crime only if they fear the inevitable negative consequences of their actions, such as returning to God, being held accountable for their actions, and the concern or fear of eternal misery in the Hereafter.

Naturally, however, such a (religious) reason is not an effective deterrent for those who do not believe in the Hereafter and the final return to God. However, one can possess a strong sense of morality and inner freedom, even without religious beliefs, which prevents one from committing such a crime. The Imam said to the enemy that if they did not have a religion reason which could prevent them from committing their crimes, then at least they could adhere to their moral compass.

You know that "ḥurriyyah" has a special meaning in our religious culture. It means inner freedom, which is something beyond outer freedom, which actually means freedom from external pressures and impositions. Inner freedom means freedom from fear and greed, and without which freedom in the truest sense cannot be achieved. (For more on different reasons for action, see Radhi, 1993: saying 237). Many of the restrictions imposed on a person by external powers are because the person does not have inner freedom; that is, in many cases, external powers impose their will on a person by taking advantage of his fear or greed. Therefore, freedom in its truest sense is achievable through inner freedom.

It is possible to oblige someone to behave according to your will without using physical force, i.e., by counting on their fear and greed. Those who intended to commit the crime in Karbala, were under the pressure of fear or greed. What Imam Hussein said to them meant that if they had inner freedom, the fear and greed that made them commit their heinous crimes, would lose their instigative power.

2.8. The Principle of Universalizability in Imam Hussein's Decisions

Shivapoor: Thank you, Dr Fanaei. My next question is about another quote of Imam Hussein which he spoke upon his departure from Medina: "Someone like me does not pledge allegiance to someone like Yazīd" (ibn Ṭāwūs. 1969: 23). Can this sentence be interpreted based on Kant's principle of universalisability? The universalisability principle states that one should act in accordance with a maxim, i.e., a guiding principle, that they can envision being universally adopted and followed by all rational agents. If we accept that saints and great people, which are regarded as ethical role models, should behave in such a way that their conduct becomes a universal law, do you think that the Imam's statement can be interpreted on the basis of this idea?

Fanaei: This is a profound question. However, some points should be considered. Firstly, it is important to avoid the fallacy of anachronism by not attributing Kant's theory, which was developed many centuries later, to Imam Hussein and thereby inadvertently giving credence to the assumption that he intended to confirm this theory. However, in today's context, we can consider Kant's moral theory and its concept of universalisability as one of the most effective frameworks available. The philosophical formulation and defence of a theory do not necessarily contradict the existence of the essence of that theory in the thoughts and consciousness of individuals who lived before it was proposed.

Secondly, the statement in question clearly implies a kind of generalisation or a general rule. There is a difference between saying, "I do not pledge allegiance to Yazīd" and "Someone like me does not pledge allegiance to someone like Yazīd". But the question is, what does the Imam mean by "like me" and "like Yazīd"? Is it about all people or a specific group of people? Kant's principle of universalisability includes all human beings or all rational beings, but does the Imam's statement mean that no human beings should pledge allegiance to a person like Yazīd when they are faced with such a situation? Or should only those who are in an exceptional position, like Imam Hussein, not do so?

In simpler terms, do Imam Hussein's unique position that influence his paying allegiance to Yazīd have any impact on whether we view this allegiance as morally, religiously and politically significant? Does it affect our assessment of whether his adversaries' aligning with Yazīd was a wrong choice? If these characteristics are involved, then the duty can only be imposed on, or expected of, people who possess those characteristics; and therefore, people who lack the same position will not be held to that standard or expectation of moral duty. Suppose someone like Yazīd wanted to force an unknown person, who does not have the specific characteristics of Imam Hussein, to pledge allegiance to him. Is such a person also morally obligated to refuse allegiance at the cost of martyrdom? That is, does the allegiance of such a person also conflict with his duty to maintain human dignity? Basically, the allegiance of such a person is not that important for Yazīd to forcibly take his allegiance.

In fact, Imam Hussein's allegiance to Yazīd would have meant recognition of the Umayyad reading of Islam and the Umayyad political theology by the grandson of the Prophet, and the religious and spiritual leader and spokesperson of 'Alawīte Islam and 'Alawīte political theology. For this reason, in another speech, Imam Hussein is quoted as saying, "When the nation of Islam becomes entangled with a leader like Yazīd, [one should bid] farewell to Islam (ibn Ṭāwūs, 1969: 24). This explains what , the Imam meant when he said that anyone in his position and as dignified as him will not swear allegiance to someone like Yazīd. Therefore, the Imam's remark cannot be generalised to all people, but still is applicable in specific contexts. That is, any person who has a position similar to, and finds themselves in a situation similar to, Imam Hussein's, where their allegiance would carry similar significance, has the moral duty not to pledge allegiance even if it leads to martyrdom. It seems that even our other Imams were not faced with situations that merited a decision like Imam Hussein's.

2.9. The Difficulty of Making Moral Decisions in Critical Situations

Shivapoor: Thank you, Dr Fanaei, for your insights. One crucial point you highlighted is that the moral lessons to be derived from the Battle of Karbala are not limited to one side of the story, i.e. the Imam and his companions. The actions of the other side, i.e. his adversaries, also present significant lessons worth considering. This historical event encompasses challenging situations where individuals face profound dilemmas, and their actions have far-reaching consequences for themselves and others. These circumstances often render wise or judicious decision-making seemingly impossible.

We have very notable examples on both sides. On Imam Hussein's side (the justice side), al-Ḥurr ibn Yazīd al-Riyāḥī, who was the commander of Yazīd's army, faces a dilemma. In the books recounting the Battle of Karbala, we come across compelling narratives that shed light on al-Ḥurr's quagmire. Overwhelmed with immense psychological stress, he grappled with his inner turmoil until a pivotal moment occurred. In the end, he made the firm decision to fully support Imam Hussein, and was martyred in the battle.

On the other side, we have Umar ibn Saʿd. According to historical reports, when offered to take command of Yazīd's army, it is reported that he anxiously paced in his room all night long, reciting poems. These poems depicted his reluctance in accepting the position, but he eventually overcame his doubts and accepted Yazīd's proposition. So my next question is, what useful lessons are there to learn from both sides of the story, which can help us make the correct moral decisions when facing dilemmas, such as when we have to choose between the bad or the worse, or between good and evil?

Fanaei: Living a moral life comes at a cost. The more significant the stakes, the more challenging the decision becomes, requiring a stronger will and a higher degree of inner freedom. The moral value of an individual is determined by the price they are willing to pay to uphold moral principles and continue to live in accordance with them. We assess our own worth based on the sacrifices we make, such as refraining from lying, oppressing others, honouring commitments, and fulfilling other moral obligations.

On one hand, there are individuals like Imam 'Ali who would not take even the husk of a grain of barley from the mouth of an ant, even if he were offered the ownership and dominion over the entire universe (Radhi, 1993: Sermon 224). On the other hand, there are people like Umar ibn Sa'd who were willing to fight against Imam Hussein for the sake of gaining control over the governorship of Ray or its vast wheatfields.

In religious terms, people are of three kinds: those who sacrifice the world for the Hereafter and to earn divine satisfaction; those who sell their Hereafter for their worldly life; and those who sell their Hereafter for others' worldly lives. In our religious literature, the term used to refer to ethical dilemmas is "affliction" (*bala*), and "test" (*ibtila*) or "divine test". In a famous saying, Imam Hussein states that:

> People are slaves of the world and religion is just an ornament on their tongues. They are committed to it as long as it provides their livelihood; therefore, when they are tested, the number of true devotees dwindles (Majlisi, 1982: 44/383).

The event of Karbala presents numerous moral dilemmas, each of which is significant and challenging, requiring individuals to make sacrifices in order to uphold their moral principles. In today's world, we are confronted with a choice between two role models: those who are willing to pay the necessary price to live morally, and those who are unwilling to make such sacrifices. This moral scale serves as a measure for everyone to evaluate their own moral values. The crucial question is, "What actions would we take if we were in Karbala and had to decide which side to join? For instance, if we were offered the governorship of Ray, an enticing proposition, would we have been able to resist the temptation?". It is easy for us to sit here today with our peace of mind and express a desire to be among those who achieved great success (Qur'ān, 4:73). However, it is important to realise that mere words hold little value. What truly matters is how we respond when are actually faced with similar situations in our own lives, when we are confronted with the need to make significant sacrifices to uphold our moral principles.

2.10. Moral Approaches and the Battle of Karbala

Shivapoor: Another question that arises when analysing the moral explanation of the Battle of Karbala is which ethical school aligns with Imam Hussein's actions? In moral philosophy, there are three main approaches: consequentialism, deontologism, and virtue ethics.

The consequentialism evaluates the morality of actions based on their morally significant outcomes. Deontologism assesses the morality of actions based on their intrinsic characteristics. On the other hand, virtue ethics focuses on the personality and character of the agent as the primary subject of evaluation.

Considering Imam Hussein's set of actions from his journey from Medina to Mecca until his martyrdom, which of the three approaches is more compatible? It is sometimes argued that religious or mystical morality, or the morality of saints and heroes are better aligned with virtue ethics, than deontologism or consequentialism. However, can we explain all of the Imam's actions solely based on virtue ethics, or do we need a combination of these approaches?

Fanaei: This is an intriguing question that can spark a lengthy discussion. However, I'll provide a brief overview of some key points. Firstly, it is important to distinguish between morality, and moral theories or different approaches in normative ethics. Morality refers to a collection of moral considerations that individuals who aspire to be moral and live morally should be aware of and adhere to. As human beings, we have always possessed intuitions about morality and recognised the importance of being virtuous and acting in accordance with those inherent ethical standards.

Ethical approaches and theories developed later. These are the result of philosophers' efforts to systematise related moral intuitions and considerations. As you said, here we have three different approaches under which the diverse moral theories can be classified. It is at this juncture that important questions are raised, including whether these three approaches are compatible with each other. And, if they are, how can we adopt them together?

Throughout the history of moral philosophy, proponents of each of these approaches have tried to criticise other approaches and defend theirs against competing ones. Over the centuries, these critiques, defences, revisions and reconstructions have resulted in complex readings of the aforementioned approaches in normative ethics, which unlike the simple readings of these approaches, are so similar to each other that it is difficult to think that they lead to different results; that is, their difference is more theoretical than practical. There is no clear boundary among them. Moreover, in recent decades a new tendency has emerged among moral philosophers, which is in fact the same synthetic and integrative approach you referred to.

I do think we can set aside these technical and philosophical debates and explain the Imam's behaviour based on all the three approaches. But first we have to accept a certain reading of these three approaches. For example, if we choose consequentialism as the framework for our explanation, we have to choose a reading of it that considers all the consequences which the Imam as the decision maker had in mind as morally important consequences. In fact, some of the Imam's decisions, actions and reactions cannot be explained if we narrow down our viewpoint to material and worldly consequences.

I think the proper reading of the consequentialism here is a version of rule-consequentialism that takes the Hereafter's consequences into account. Also, it should recognise the principle of justice, and the value of human dignity and honour martyrdom as a morally good kind of death; one that is

63

preferable to life without dignity. This reading of consequentialism is also compatible with a certain reading of deontologism. It is also possible to consider the moral considerations evident in this event, which are formulated as moral principles in rule-consequentialism and deontologism, as moral virtues of the moral agent, and thus, attributing these moral properties to the Imam and his companions as moral virtues.

2.11. Mourning from a Moral Point of View

Shivapoor: Dr Fanaei, my questions so far were all about the event itself, its explanations, and the lessons it provides us with. But we Shi'as have been performing Muharram mourning rituals for centuries in response to this event. My next question is, what kind of mourning is morally justified in general, and what kind of mourning for saints and moral heroes like Imam Hussein is morally acceptable? There is no doubt that mourning is a religious practice. It is one of our important religious rituals which serves to define Twelver Shi'a communal identity. But is mourning a morally correct reaction? In other words, what are, or should be, the characteristics of the moral mourning?

Fanaei: This is a pertinent question indeed. First let me present a clearer formulation of the question, if I may. Your question in fact seems to be, "Do we have a moral reason to mourn or not?" As you've already said, we have a religious reason for mourning for Imam Hussein, and the Ahl al-Bayt in general, but do we also have a moral – meta-religious – reason that shows mourning is morally obligatory or only recommended?

It seems that, under certain conditions, mourning is a morally good and right thing to do. However, the assessment of those conditions necessitates further consideration. In other words, mourning is a voluntary behaviour that is subject to moral evaluation. The set of moral considerations related to mourning could be grouped under the title of "The Ethics of Mourning".

2.12. The Instrumental Value of Mourning and the Condition for its Moral Justification

From a religious and moral point of view, it is clear that mourning has no intrinsic value and desirability; its value comes from something beyond it, that is, from a goal which is intrinsically valuable. This serves as our point of departure for the evaluation of mourning from a moral point of view.

Therefore, mourning for the sake of mourning is meaningless; in addressing the question of moral value of mourning, there are two preliminary questions that must be answered first: "Mourning for whom?", and "Mourning for what purpose?"

On the one hand, the value of mourning depends on how well we know the person for whom we are mourning. If the mourner has an imaginary, illusory, or superstitious image of Imam Hussein in mind, then their mourning will lose its value. In other words, if the image of Imam Hussein is distorted in the mind of the mourner, they are not the true mourner of Imam Hussein, or as we say, they are crying over a grave in which there is no corpse, or contains some other dead body in it. Therefore, the value of mourning for Imam Hussein is completely dependent on how accurate and undistorted knowledge and understanding we have about him. Thus, any distortion of facts in the narration of the event of Karbala in mourning rituals merely for the purpose of arousing people's emotions and making them cry, renders the mourning vain.

On the other hand, the goal that makes mourning for Imam Hussein valuable is the moral and profound spiritual transformation of the mourners' personality and conduct. This is because the act of grieving would hold extrinsic value solely when it serves as a catalyst for personal growth, such as: being consistently honest and with wisdom, being fair in public and private dealings, being respectful of others' and the self's rights, being forgiving and merciful, keeping material wealth only as much as is needful, and being generous towards others.

However, in the case of mourning for Imam Hussein, I would go further: in my view, the main purpose of mourning has always been to keep alive the 'Alawīte reading of Islam by forming an existential bond between the griever and Imam Hussein as the role model of the 'Alawīte reading of Islam. Therefore, for the mourner the moral value of grieving depends entirely on perceiving Imam Hussein as a moral and spiritual role model. However, as stated before, regrettably the commemoration of Imam Hussein, like various rituals in Islam and other religions, has been subjected to distortions throughout history, leading to unintended consequences. Nowadays, sarcastically speaking, it would seem that mourning serves as a green light for those who live according to the Umayyad reading of Islam throughout the year, and then participate in Muharram gatherings for ten night to relieve their guilty conscience, thinking that shedding tears will lead to the forgiveness of their sins – but without any change occurring in their personality, behaviour and/or lifestyle. From this perspective, perhaps mourning is the same as other forms of worship and religious rituals. The purpose of the daily prayers, for example, is to restrain the worshiper from indecent and wrongful conduct in life. Therefore, a prayer that does not have such characteristics or does not perform such a function, fails to fulfil the moral conditions, even if it is legally valid from a jurisprudential perspective. If the purpose of mourning is something else, or if it, as Sharīʿatī (1988: 235-236), says, "turns blood into opium", Yazīd and his followers may well be willing to participate in the mourning rituals.

Thus, the original purpose of mourning for Imam Hussein is to renew our allegiance to him as a role model; the goal is to keep alive his way of life in our minds and hearts so that by the time the grieving period ends, it can play an active role in our life and death. If we are the kind of people who ask Imam Hussein for help and cherish his memory in the rituals, but act in our daily life as if our role model is Yazīd, then certainly we have lost our way. In other words, grieving for Imam Hussein is, in a way, grieving for the preservation of the values he sacrificed his life for, ensuring they are not disregarded. Our admiration for him signifies our devotion to those very principles he laid down his life for.

2.13. The Ethics of Mourning

Shivapoor: What good points you made! My next question is, if mourning is supposed to be a form of worship, what moral values should be considered and observed in mourning to practice living a moral life? For example, sometimes it is rightly said that mourning should not hurt others, such as the sound emanated by the speakers should not cause noise pollution; extravagance should be avoided in the votive offerings, etc. In your opinion, which moral principles should be observed in mourning itself? Is there something as "ethics of mourning"? If yes, what would be these principles?

Fanaei: Yes, there is no doubt that moral principles can be applied to mourning, because it is a voluntary action, and like all other voluntary actions, it too is subject to moral evaluation. However, we need to distinguish two categories of moral values: One encompasses the values pertaining to social morality, as you previously noted a few illustrative examples, while the other focuses on the values associated with personal morality. But what items the complete list of relevant moral values includes requires a more detailed study and investigation. In fact, it may be possible to propose the ethics of mourning as one of the branches of Applied Ethics and see what the general and fundamental moral principles are required when they are applied to this case. Actually, I do not have any special moral principle in mind now other than the ones mentioned earlier. Nevertheless, I would like to mention some preliminary points that should be considered in any research on mourning ethics.

The first point, which I also mentioned earlier, is that we should think of mourning as a means and not as an end. Based on this assumption, instrumental rationality requires us to answer these questions: "Does this means lead us to our goal?", and "Is this the best possible and available means to reach that goal?"

To put it more clearly, we should see mourning as a form of worship since in its truest essence, it is a means of increasing people's morality and spirituality. This is an achievable goal, and it has an objective reality: the person who worships should become more moral and spiritual in this world, and this transformation should be noticeable both for the person and others. According to the Qur'ān, important forms of worship such as the daily prayers, fasting, and pilgrimage have instrumental value – their purpose is to enhance the moral and spiritual growth of the individual who performs them.

For example, regarding prayer, Allah says, "… Indeed the prayer restrains from indecent and wrongful conduct…" (Qur'ān, 29:45). Therefore, if a person prays, but the ritual does not prevent them from indecent and wrongful conduct, it may be that their performance of the prayer is not the kind that the Qur'ān prescribes. Likewise, about fasting, He says, "Prescribed for you is fasting as it was prescribed for those who were before you, so that you may be God-wary" (Qur'ān, 2:183); and about the ritual animal sacrifice performed during Hajj, "It is not their flesh or blood that reaches Allāh.

Rather, it is your piety that reaches Him" (Qur'ān 22:37). This would show that, when viewed from a Divine perspective, all these forms of worship are purposeful and have two goals: one is moral and the other is spiritual.

These two goals must be achieved in this world and before death. If they are not met, it will be clear that our worship is not the recommended form of worship by God in the Qur'ān, and that there may be no rewards associated with it. Mourning is no exception to this rule. Unfortunately, it would seem that today many mourning rituals do not tend to correspond to the glory of Imam Hussein, nor do they seem to have the desirable lofty effects on the people performing them. Rather, it would appear to some that they are forms of unconscious or subconscious entertainment and frenzied expressions. Certainly, this is not what our Imams bore in mind when the practiced and preached about grieving for Imam Hussein.

Shivapoor: I thank Dr Fanaei for his precious time. I myself learned a lot from this conversation and I hope it would be useful for the audience as well. Dr Fanaei, is there anything else you want to add or share with our audience?

Fanaei: Thank you for your great questions and for your efforts in making this happen. I'd also like to thank the production crew, and the respected audiences.

CHAPTER THREE

Common Explanations about the Battle of Karbala

3.1. Introduction

Let me start by expressing my condolences on the Arbaʿeen[4] of Hussein ibn Ali, the chief of the martyrs. The occasion necessitates us talking about the philosophy behind his uprising. According to Moṭahhari, the history of Karbala has two pages: one bright, the other dark. From one perspective, Karbala is the display of human crimes and offences (Moṭahhari 1969: p. 35). In today's parlance, it would be regarded as a crime against humanity, as the brutality meted out then is either rare or unparalleled, ranging from the massacre of the innocent to the act of killing an infant; denying the oppressed group water; trampling corpses under the hooves of military horses; decapitating heads of the dead and mounting them on spears; setting fire to the tents of non-combatants; plundering, scourging women and kids within them; and pitching battalions against a group of just seventy-two – which included trained and untrained young and old men. This is the dark side of the history of Karbala, and its worldly heroes are Yazīd, Umar ibn Saʿd, Shimr, and their rank and file. This dark page strongly represents the brutal and bestial nature of the human being. Upon reading this dark page, everyone ends up in nothing but damnation, imprecation, and breaking into tears, and threnody.

On the other hand, the bright page of the history of Karbala is the demonstration of honour and beauty; and the

---

[4] The 40th day after ʿĀshūrā.

glorious manifestation of supreme human virtues such as sacrifice and devotion; and of the sublime potential of the human self. Considered a school of morality, the bright page tells us how to live and die. The protagonists of this page are Imam Hussein, his noble family and his loyal, self-sacrificing companions. Here, we witness humanity at its peak.[5]

The Battle of Karbala has frequently been distorted throughout the history, yet the most glaring distortion – which concerns the understanding of this event and can be seen as the root of other distortions—occurs due to paying excessive attention to the dark page of the history of Karbala and ignoring the bright one.[6] The question is, what should we do if we want to read the bright page of the history of Karbala? In other words, what shall we do if we really want to have Imam Hussein as our role model transforming our character and conduct both in this life and beyond?

3.2. How to Understand the Battle of Karbala and Beware of Distortion

The first thing to do is achieve a true understanding of the very concept of Karbala. The endeavour would inevitably require a

---

[5] Reconsidering the conventional way, Motahhari (1969: pp. 301–334) raises the questions as to why we must always look at the dark page of the Battle of Karbala too; why we always narrate the crimes occurred there;, why we always study Imam Hussein as the victim of the criminals; why our mottos in the name of Hussein are derived from the dark page of Karbala. That the Shia are more interested in reading the dark page of the history of Karbala rather than its bright page has various cultural, social, and political reasons, which calls for sociological research.

[6] For instance, Rumi is among the few who invite us to view the Battle of Karbala from this perspective. See pages 139–165 in Soroush (2000).

profound explanation of the event if the aim is to learn for the sake of improving one's conduct, words and attitudes about how to live and die. By "explanation", I mean the explication of the cause, which entails referring to its underlying factors such as the goal and motivation of those who played a role in triggering the event.

The identification of the causes of an event has both theoretical and practical advantages. The former helps with the question of *why*, thus making clear the reasons for the occurrence, as well as providing possible insights into what measures can be adopted to prevent its recurrence. Conversely, it may also allow for the enablement of a favourable event by practically creating its underlying causes.

The above-mentioned point holds true for the explanation of both natural and human events. There is a significant difference between these in that the latter is the effect of human volitional action, be it individual or collective, which they make in line with their beliefs and values. Thus, the explanation of human phenomena involves the philosophy of action and the fundamentals of human agency.

3.3. Causes of Historical Events

The events caused by direct human intervention have various underlying factors, which can be listed in three general categories:

1) *Context*: The situational factors – with "context" used in a general sense of the word – presuppose that human action is actually a response to environmental circumstances. No behaviour exists as *a priori* and as completely detached from

its relevant circumstances – a comprehensive understanding of these would be necessary to offer accurate explanations of the events and people's behaviours. As the Battle of Karbala is no exception to this, it is not possible to offer its true explanation without delving into its cultural, political, and historical context.

2) *Beliefs*: The beliefs of the actors within an event constitute an important factor. For example, a person's deep faith and belief in God and the afterlife can help them to not fear the death and, if necessary, sacrifice their life for the sake of an eminent ideal, and accept martyrdom – that is, prefer death with dignity over a life of abasement because such a person knows that they lose nothing with their death. According to Rumi, such a person never feels the loss of significance due to death as for them, it is tantamount to a yet further life onto the route towards spiritual excellence and perfection. In other words, their death in this realm to them is merely the release of the spirit from the prison of the material world into an ethereal realm.

3) *Norms and Values*: Virtues, values, norms, and dos and don'ts inculcated by an individual within themselves dictate their behaviour in a particular situation or context; and in instances of conflict within their norms and senses of duty, decide which they deem important, which ones they can sacrifice in lieu.

3.4. Desirable Explanation of the Battle of Karbala

Each of the above factors is important with regards to the Battle of Karbala. However, what we seek here is to grasp the rationale that governed Imam Hussein's behaviour. We want to know what system of values and norms he followed as a rational agent who played an influential role in the event; what virtues oriented him; and on the basis of what principles he made his decisions and actions. If those principles are universalisable to include other similar circumstances and individuals, it would mean that we should be obliged to adopt them in similar circumstances that we might face. Moreover, if those principles are to be regarded as moral, it would mean that Imam Hussein is a living school and a role model of morality for humanity at large, and not just for the Shi'a or Muslims in general.

Imam Hussein says, "I am a role model for you" (Abu Mikhnaf al-Kufi, 1996: p. 172). By this statement, he means that he follows a set of principles in his conduct, which are not exclusive to himself and can be generalised to include all those who live in a similar context. Therefore, the central question is, what kind of reason did Imam Hussein follow to make decisions and act accordingly? Is it something mysterious that cannot be grasped and thus incapable of being followed? Or is it a combination of mystical, political, jurisprudential (*fiqhi*) and/or moral reasons? These can be regarded as sets of normative and axiological principles that are supposed to direct the behaviour and decision-making of rational agents empowered with free will.

To be considered as conveying such a message and lesson, the Battle of Karbala requires a natural, terrestrial and human explanation that could justify Imam Hussein's actions on the basis of the wisdom found in all humans to a greater or lesser degree. Thus, the mythical, metaphysical, extraterrestrial and the superhuman explanations will not have such a quality. By these explanations, I mean those that attempts to explain the event by referring to unseen and supernatural causes and the exclusive characteristics of Imam Hussein, such as his infallibility (*'iṣmah*) and knowledge of the unseen.

3.5. The Metaphysical/Mythical Explanation of the Battle of Karbala

Up until recent decades, the prevailing understanding among the Shi'a has been the view that Imam Hussein's movement does not lend itself to scientific and rational explanation, hence, it is incapable of being adequately discussed, adopted and followed by the mass of humanity. In this case, the orthodox view holds that Imam Hussein's uprising is a hidden secret which does not follow a rational reason, and that we just know that the death of Imam Hussein was in line with the Divine Providence. In this perspective, the devotional martyrdom is related merely to an excusive personal command, and the possibility that there were some rational grounds for the Imam's own volition in his decision-making and actions is ruled out. This view emphasises the role played by the Imam's knowledge of the unseen and the Divine predetermination (Ṣāliḥī Najafābādī, 1970: p. 10).[7]

In Iran's contemporary history, Ali Sharī'atī emerged as a prominent thinker who sought to provide a rational and humanistic interpretation of the Battle of Karbala. Unlike met-

---

[7] For a detailed analysis of this explanation, see Ṣāliḥī Najafābādī (1988: p. 9.) and Moṭahhari (1998).

aphysical and mythical explanations, Sharīʿatī proposed a more tangible understanding of the event: that the interplay of three factors – wealth, power, and duplicity – converged to transform blood into opium (Sharīʿatī, 1988: pp. 235–236). In this framework, or proposition, blood symbolises life, movement and resistance, while opium represents death, silence, apathy, lethargy and submission in the face of oppression and power. Thus, this raises the question: "How can 'blood' undergo such a transformation into 'opium'?"

My answer to this question is: "Through providing a supernatural or metaphysical or mythical explanation insisting upon the will of God while ignoring the role of human agency". Regarding the event of Karbala, it is said that Imam Hussein's martyrdom was divine destiny; a destiny that had been known since the beginning of creation, and before his birth, the Prophet, his mother and his father were aware of it, and Imam Hussein himself had foreknowledge of it. Therefore, Imam Hussein knew in advance exactly when and where he would be martyred, and based on his knowledge of the unseen, he moved towards his inevitable fate and in his behaviour was merely an unwilling executor of God's predetermined will.

Prior to Sharīʿatī's initiative, this explanation was the prevailing conception among the Shiʿa; in fact, it is still accepted by many followers. In truth, accepting the metaphysical explanation produces no benefit except some religious rituals such as mourning, threnody, chest beating and self-flagellation (*tatbir*).

Disregarding the didactic, awakening, stimulating and redemptive aspect of the Battle of Karbala, the metaphysical explanation fails to provide guidance on how to live and die. It presents the Battle of Karbala as a unique case where the Imam's behaviour either lacked a discernible rationale or followed an undecipherable reason, making it impossible to follow him as a role model.

3.6. Criticism of the Metaphysical Explanation

The metaphysical explanation is not entirely wrong as it bears some truth supported by evidence in the historical sources of narrations. For example, one of them is, "Allāh determined to see thee dead" (ibn Ṭāwūs, 1969, p. 65).[8]

However, the error in the metaphysical explanation lies in the fact that it is by no means an explanation since Divine Will is invariably relevant in every natural phenomenon. In this sense, if Imam Hussein had not been martyred, it would

---

[8] In his book *Shahid-e Javid* [The Eternal Martyr], Ṣāliḥī Najafābādī fully discusses and criticises the narration as "fake" (Ṣāliḥī Najafābādī, 1970: pp. 120–136). Moreover, Mahdi Simaei, in chapter five of *Mashhurat-e Bi-ete-bar dar Tarikh* [Popular Invalid Statements in History], examines and criticises the hadith associated with this narration alongside other ones about the Battle of Karbala, showing that the narration quoted lacks validity. Even in its absence, the martyrdom of Imam Husayn could be seen as governed by Divine Will to see him dead in the battle because according the Tawhidi perspective, the occurrence of any event is necessarily in line with Divine creative (*takwini*) Providence and Will in the universe. Therefore, concerning this narration as well as other similar ones, it is possible to offer interpretations based on free will since the general compatibility of divine providence with human volition also holds true for our case here. Ayatollah Motahhari understands the providence inherent in this narration neither as creative nor individual legislative (*tashri'i*) but as the "general legislative will or Sharia-based providence of Allah" (Motahhari, 1998: pp. 471–472). In contrast, Ṣāliḥī Najafābādī (1970: p. 128) believes that the providence in this narration can be viewed "neither as the Divine creative nor as divine legislative will".

also have been due to Divine Will and Providence. There-fore, while the metaphysical explanation carries some phil-osophical and theological merit, it is *invariably* relevant to the cases of occurrence or non-occurrence. This is because any event in the natural world has a natural and scientific ex-planation, which is *variably* relevant to the occurrence and non-occurrence of the event.

Further, it cannot be concluded from this explanation that Imam Hussein was compelled and overpowered by Di-vine Will in this event, and that he did not make decisions and act based on his own intellect and information availa-ble to him through normal and human epistemic channels. Such a conclusion, if valid, would mean that the Imam's as well as his companions' conduct does not deserve praise and admiration, nor is the behaviour of Yazīd and his army repre-hensible. This supposition equally views both parties as just entities executing Allāh's Will and lacking individual volition and responsibility. Moreover, there is some historical docu-ments that do not support the metaphysical explanation. For example, Imam Hussein frequently advised Yazīd's army not to commit any crime, or that he somehow decided to return to Medina or divert to Yemen following the news of the mar-tyrdom of Muslim ibn 'Aqīl. In other words, the metaphysical explanation seems to be more in tune with the determinism as a fundamental principle of Umayyad Islam rather than with those of 'Alawīte Islam which are based on the idea of free will.

Nevertheless, upon the occurrence of any event, it is easy to reason that God would like it that particular way and we can do nothing before His Will, except by submission to it.

This form of reasoning would be tantamount to eschewing moral responsibility and criticism. It dismisses the role of human beings' volition, capacity to reason, wisdom and responsibility, as well as the contextual factors that may influence the occurrence of a given event – all because they are seen as subordinate to Divine Will. Accordingly, it would not be possible to learn lessons from the Battle of Karbala, and mourning for Imam Hussain and damnation of Yazīd would be the only conceivable reaction, and achievements.

The insistence of some Shiʿa to adhere to the metaphysical explanation correspondingly give Imam Hussein a status that is similar to that attached to Jesus by some Christians. Effectively, the former also subscribe to the view that Imam Hussein was killed so that they could cry for him and thus, receive forgiveness for their sins. This reasoning should not be considered an explanation but a distortion, which, in Sharīʿatī's words, transforms blood into opium. Such a metaphysical reasoning is actually welcomed by tyrannical and despotic regimes because it helps entertain the masses, keeps or makes them ignorant, distracts them from logical reasoning, responsibility, and self-accountability.[9]

Another reasoning similar to the metaphysical-cum-mythical explanation is to say that Imam Hussein acted according

---

[9] According to the historical evidence, Yazīd was the first who attempted to use some Qurʾānic verses in order to offer this explanation about the Battle of Karbala. In the meeting where the Karbala captives were present and the decapitated head of Imam Hussein was placed before him, Yazīd said, "Do you know why this disaster happened to him? Because he had not understood the religion very well, and he had not read the Qurʾānic verse saying: "Oh Allāh, you are the owner of the Empire, and you give it to and take it away from anyone you want" (Ṭabari as cited in Ṣāliḥī Najafābādī, 1970: pp. 29–33).

to an exclusive command from Allāh that is not generalisable to other human beings (Najafābādī, 1970: pp. 10–11; Motahhari, 1998: pp. 472–474).

3.7. Sharīʿatī's Political Explanation

As I mentioned, perhaps among Shiʿa thinkers, Sharīʿatī was the first person who tried to provide a rational, earthly and natural explanation of this event, based on which Imam Hussein's actions and reactions in this event can be regarded as relatable and exemplary for humanity to learn from, and determine their way of life and death accordingly.

The novel explanation offered by Sharīʿatī can be summarised as follows: On the basis of his accurate information about the historical and sociopolitical circumstances of the time obtained through the conventional sources of knowledge available to everyone, Imam Hussein knew that the uprising against the Umayyads would not yield the desirable result; that is, the overthrow of the tyrannical and despotic caliphate founded on hereditary rule, and then the establishment of a just political system based on *Imamate*. Therefore, Imam Hussein was not duty-bound to perform *jihad* since it is conditional upon having power and capability. The only thing he could do was to undertake the task of disclosing the corrupt and illegitimate face of the Umayyad Caliphate through his martyrdom. This disclosure was the only purpose of Imam Hussein, and he did succeed in achieving his goal.

According to Sharīʿatī, Imam Hussein followed a specific axiological and normative principle, articulating that if you can kill, then kill; if you cannot kill, then die (Sharīʿatī, 1988:

p. 195). It means that if a person can succeed in *jihad* and the uprising against tyrannical and dictatorial rule, they should undertake the obligation of *jihad* and overthrow of the unjust ruler. However, if a person cannot embark on it or knows that it is going to be fruitless, they are no longer charged with the responsibility of *jihad* but with the task of exposure of the oppressor through martyrdom.

For Sharīʿatī, the sociopolitical and cultural circumstances of the time had made it impossible for the fight against the Umayyad Caliphate to become successful. Therefore, the only thing Imam Hussein could do was to reveal the notorious nature of the Umayyad regime and awaken the conscience of Muslims through martyrdom. Of course, when ignorance leaves the masses, they may finally rebel and overthrow the tyrannical and dictatorial rule. However, even if martyrdom does not have such a political achievement, it will at least have this great accomplishment of tearing off the mask of sanctity and religious legitimacy that the Umayyad system had put on its face, calling itself the Caliphate of God, and its rulers the Prophet's successors.

Therefore, Sharīʿatī thinks that right from the outset of his departure from Medina, Imam Hussein was motivated by the sole purpose of martyrdom. Sharīʿatī concluded that that we have a similar duty in similar conditions. If we cannot kill the oppressor, then at least we can fight and die and thus, unmask them. For Sharīʿatī, martyrdom is a duty for those who know that their *jihad* will be unsuccessful.

Comparing his explanation with the contrasting explanations, Sharīʿatī illustrates its superiority thus:

[...] the theory of *Shahīd-e Javid* (The Eternal Martyr) which interprets the mission of ʿAshura as an uprising and jihad to destroy Yazid's [political] regime, is more positive and progressive than the Safavid-Sufi-Christian style of martyrdom, which is the biggest "friendly" conspiracy against ʿAshura and Imam Hussein, because this theory considers Imam Hussein's uprising a failed jihad, like the [Battle of] Uhud led by the Prophet or the war against Muʿawiya led by Imam Hasan. However, my theory that "martyrdom" in its specific sense in Islam is a "rule" after "jihad" and the martyr comes to the scene when the warrior is defeated, is a superior, more progressive and more justifiable theory than the theory [viewing] of [Imam] Hussein's uprising as a failed attempt. (Sharīʿatī, 1988: p. 189).

3.8. Criticism of Sharīʿatī's Political Explanation

Sharīʿatī's explanation has its own pros and cons. His explanation is helpful in that it is in accordance with some historical evidence and data, and it explains them very well. For instance, his explanation satisfactorily addresses the question as to why on his perilous journey, Imam Hussein, took the women and children of the Ahl al-Bayt, such as lady Zaynab, although he knew, relying on the rational foresight, that they would probably be taken captive. This question is not satisfactorily addressed by other explanations, yet Sharīʿatī's response that "every revolution has two faces: blood and message" (Sharīʿatī, 1988: p. 203), and the mission which shaped the Battle of Karbala had two parts: while Imam Hussein and other martyrs undertook the first part, the Karbala captives, led by lady Zaynab, were tasked with the second.

For Sharī'atī, mere martyrdom does not suffice to disclose the face of the despotic rule, and after martyrdom, there must be some figures who convey the message of the martyrs' blood to the masses. This is why he states that those who survived in the battle, carried on the remainder of Imam Hussein's mission, while the supporters and believers in the cause of Imam Hussein in the years since, must continue lady Zaynab's, otherwise they may be regarded as followers of Yazīd (Sharī'atī, 1988: p. 208).

However, Sharī'atī's explanation carries some defects. First, it is incompatible with some historical data. For example, his explanation does not satisfactorily answer the questions as to why Imam Hussein left Medina for Mecca and then diverted towards Kufa, or why Muslim ibn 'Aqīl was dispatched to Kufa to ascertain the allegiance of people of Kufa to Imam Hussein and obtain first-hand accounts about the situation in Kufa. The argument for this is that for the one whose purpose is martyrdom right from the beginning would not necessarily need to move to Kufa and accept the Kufians' invitation – in fact, there might be better places for the person to go achieve his martyrdom.

Second, as Soroush notes in a speech,[10] Sharī'atī's desirable result – that all people should die if they cannot kill – cannot be derived from his explanation because every form or endeavour towards martyrdom is different from Imam Hussein's in terms of context. Imam Hussein was unique. As the grandson of the Prophet, people knew the Prophet loved him immensely, and that the Imam had a lofty social

---

[10] To the best of my knowledge, this speech has not been published in print.

status and dignity in the land. In ibn Abbas's words, "people were with him in heart, although their swords were against him" (Arbali, 1961: p. 43). Such an individual's martyrdom can change the society and awaken the subdued conscience of people, but the martyrdom of other individuals may not necessarily have the same effects.

Therefore, Sharīʿatī's explanation would at most lead to the conclusion that if one's social status and dignity would guarantee the awakening of people's conscience, then that person should perform the duty of exposure-of-the-evil through martyrdom.

3.9. Ṣāliḥī Najafābādī's Political Explanation

The second contemporary natural-cum-scientific explanation about the Battle of Karbala was offered by Ṣāliḥī Najafābādī, an innovative jurist from the Qom Seminary. He published his research attempt in a *sui generis* book entitled *Shahid-e Javid* (The Eternal Martyr). Although one may not agree with the conclusions drawn by Najafābādī, his method of examination and analysis of historical data is admirable.

In the introduction to his book, Najafābādī categorises the explanations about the Battle of Karbala into two groups thus:

> Among the writers who have commented on Imam Hussein ibn Ali's uprising against Yazīd, we see two groups that have fallen into the two extremes of excess and negligence, whose opinions are directly opposed to each other and stand at two opposite poles. One group of Sunnis considers Imam Hus-

sein's uprising an immature, ill-planned and unsuccessful rebellion against the ruling government, and attributes error to the Imam in this uprising. The logic of this group is this: Hussein ibn Ali (AS), without having military and financial power and without a proper plan, and without perfect political arrangement and precise diplomatic tactics, rebelled against Yazīd's strong government, disrupted public order, and forced the government apparatus to suppress his rebellion in order to establish social order and security, as per the order of the Prophet: 'Whoever wants to divide the affairs of this nation while it is united, strike him with the sword no matter who he is.'[11]

Therefore, Hussein ibn Ali (AS) himself is responsible for the horrific incident of Karbala.

And opposite this group, a number of Shiʻa writers have taken the Imam's uprising out of the framework of rational measures and legal principles, and considered it following a special and hidden divine plan and order, and said: Imam Hussein (AS), by following the knowledge of Imamate – which is a branch of private sciences – and by virtue of a confidential divine order, initiated this unprecedented uprising, and no one has the right to comment or question the Imam's action.[12]

According to this group, it is better that we do not say anything about this issue and do not investigate it and leave the knowledge of such matters to the Imam himself. (1970: pp. 9–10).

Evaluating the two viewpoints, Najafābādī continues:

---

[11] *al-Awasim Min al-Ghawasim*, p. 232.

[12] *Bihar al-Anwar*, vol. 10, p. 215.

Obviously, with this logic, Hussein ibn Ali's uprising takes on the colour of a miraculous act and goes beyond the reach of others to benefit from, and loses the potential for following and utilisation, because according to this belief, the order for the Imam's uprising was a confidential divine order that no one can be aware of, and no one other than himself can understand his goal.

On this logic, Hussein ibn Ali (AS) had a divine order to kill himself and thereby attain great reward,[13] and no one has the right to discuss or question this.

It goes without saying that if we accept either of these two contradictory views about the Imam's uprising, we cannot follow and benefit from it. [...] In our opinion, the proponents of these two contradictory views, since they considered the Imam's uprising a naïve move in all its stages, and meanwhile thought that he did not have adequate army in any of the stages of the uprising, and on the other hand they saw that a naïve uprising without adequate army is not a wise act, therefore those who did not believe in Hussein ibn Ali's Imamate and infallibility have naturally attributed error to the Imam in this uprising!

And those who believed in his imamate and infallibility, since they could not reconcile his movement with rational criteria, have had no choice but to say: "the Imam's act was a special act done on the basis of a confidential and hidden divine order, and no one has the right to discuss or follow his uprising! (ibid: p. 9–12).

---

[13] *Lahuf*, p. 23. *Lahuf*'s phrase is: "Attaining martyrdom by divine order is one of the highest degrees of felicity."

Najafābādī then briefly expounds on his own viewpoint:

> However, in contrast to the two previous views, there is another perspective which accepts both the secret divine command and considers the Imam's actions as worthy of following and emulating. This is because whatever the secret command may have been, his holiness acted upon it, and the Imam's actions generally serve as a model and guide for others who should take it as a pattern for their own conduct (except in cases where there is definitive evidence that a particular action of the Imam was an exclusive duty for him alone).
>
> From our comprehensive examination of this subject, we have concluded that the movement of Imam Hussein (peace be upon him) was a rational, necessary, and unavoidable action even from the perspective of intellectual traditions and legal and social laws. (*ibid.*)

Najafābādī presupposes that the Imam's uprising can be analysed and explained on the basis of evaluations of natural human reason and the information accessible to the Imam through ordinary sources of knowledge. This is why some orthodox critics have accused Najafābādī of denying the Imam's knowledge of the unseen. In Najafābādī's explanation, Imam Hussein carried out the uprising in order to overthrow Yazīd's rule and establish an Islamic state. Concerning the letters and invitations of the Kufians delivered to Imam Hussein, there was greater likelihood that the uprising could be successful – which can help explain the Imam's uprising on rational grounds. However, the circumstances turned unfavourable, and the Imam's prediction turned out to be wrong.

As a result, he reluctantly acquiesced to the imposed war, and was finally martyred, although he never stopped dissuading the enemy from committing the grave crime. Therefore, martyrdom was imposed upon Imam Hussein (*ibid.*).

3.10. Criticism of Ṣāliḥī Najafābādī's Political Explanation

Najafābādī offers some important points worthy of further consideration. For example, he makes a distinction between "the confidentiality of the divine command based on knowledge of the unseen" and "the exclusiveness of the duty called by that command". The distinction shows not only Najafābādī's belief in the Imam's knowledge of the unseen but also his stance that the contents of the divine command are not exclusive to the Imam.

However, it seems that the above distinction cannot justify Najafābādī's desired conclusion since it is incompatible with one of the theological presuppositions widely accepted by Shiʿa scholars: that any change in religious rules is no longer possible or allowable following the death of Prophet Muhammad and the ensuing finality of prophecy, and Imams only perform to propagate and explicate previously fixed religious rules. As such, that the Imam received a new secret command from Allāh containing a new religious rule for Muslims is not compatible with the concept of the finality of prophecy because it is supposed that the command is not derived from the adaptation of general rules, which were already delivered by the Prophet – otherwise it could not be secret or unseen. Moreover, this would contradict the Imam's explanation of his reasons given to public audiences, including friends and foes, where he argues that his movement is by no means a *bid'ah* (innovation in religious matters), but it is based on the teachings of Prophet Muhammad and Imam 'Ali.

In my opinion, the Imam's knowledge of the unseen should be treated differently. The content of his knowledge of the unseen is either a *command* to embark on an uprising and martyrdom or *information* about martyrdom. The former renders the command as not based on a new religious rule but on the principles already provided in the Qur'ān and the life of the Prophet and Imams. However, in the case of knowledge of the unseen as the information about martyrdom, the doctrine of *badā'* warrants the claim that the information about martyrdom is equal to the information about the contingent divine predestination. This is why Imam Hussein never stopped advising his foes and dissuading them from their grave crime. If his advice had found a way into their hardened hearts, and if they had abandoned the idea of killing him, it would have been clear that *badā'* was proved for Allāh instead – which is compatible with the Imam's knowledge of the unseen.

The second point in Najafābādī's explanation is the attempt at combining the metaphysical explanation (based on knowledge of the unseen) and terrestrial explanation (based on ordinary sources of knowledge). However, concerning the latter explanation, which is the focus of his book, Najafābādī tries to prove the rationality of Imam Hussein's movement by showing its compatibility with the traditions of reason, and legal and social rules.

However, what seems to be missing in Najafābādī's explanation and in almost all other explanations, is the role of morality, moral rationality, and moral values and duties in explaining Imam Hussein's decision and (re)action. Why not say that Imam Hussein acted according to his moral duty, that his movement from beginning to end, was based on moral values?

Najafābādī's explanation has its advantages and disadvantages. Concerning the former, it covers and explains some historical data about the Battle of Karbala. For example, the Imam's departure from Medina for Kufa; his talks with the heads of Yazīd's army – wherein he referred to the letters of invitation sent to him by the Kufians as his reason to proceed towards Kufa; his speech about his motivation before and after leaving Medina in which he talked about enjoining right and forbidding wrong; and his questioning of the legitimacy of Yazīd's rule.

However, Najafābādī's explanation suffers from the disadvantage that it does not harmonise with some other historical data, or that it even fails to elaborate them. For instance, it does not satisfactorily answer the question as to why Imam Hussein did not surrender to the enemy and instead preferred martyrdom over making an oath of allegiance to Yazīd, when ostensibly, he would have known all along about the martyrdom of Muslim ibn ʿAqīl and the subsequent disinclination and cowardice of the Kufians to rise in his support. The explanation also does not address the reason why the followers of Imam Hussein in Kufa, who were supposedly in the majority, were easily frightened and surrendered due to the intimidation of the minority in a way that all of them dispersed and abandoned Muslim ibn ʿAqīl to be finally arrested and martyred.

Moreover, Najafābādī presupposes that Imam Hussein's

ultimate goal was to establish an Islamic state and implement Islamic jurisprudential rules (*fiqh*). It is actually considered that the implementation of religious rules depends on the establishment of a specific state responsible for enjoining citizens to do right and forbidding them from doing wrong. This is the very conception that is found among most Islamists and religious fundamentalists. In this conception, the Islamic society becomes corrupt, with the corruption being equal to the abandonment or infringement of religious rules by lay people. According to them, in order to eliminate the corruption, an Islamic state should be established that implements the religious rules and ensures the masses obey those rules. In other words, the state is actually considered as an instrument to implement religious rules, and that Imam Hussein's uprising was intended to serve the same purpose.

However, adhering to a misguided presupposition about the root of political corruption, the above conception of the relationship between religion and politics entirely overlooks the important role the civil religion plays through the civil society in preventing the corruption. The state itself is the most important institution in every society, including the religious, that becomes corrupt and needs to be reformed. Since the state is the most influential and powerful social institution, any corruption therein leads to the corruption of its citizens as well as other institutions. It is not possible to prevent the state corruption by replacing agents of the same; instead, it may be eliminated through a powerful civil society.

If enjoining right and forbidding wrong is to prevent corruption, which is actually the case, it must be the responsibility of civil society towards the state, and not vice versa.

Thus, enjoining right and forbidding wrong would more aptly mean to prevent the corruption of rulers and state institutions.

In other words, people are obliged to prevent the corruption of rulers and state institutions by constantly monitoring and criticising their performance, thus preventing government officials from damnation due to their advertent or inadvertent abuse of power and wealth, and neglect their responsibilities. However, there is a very naïve conception of political power and its requirements, according to which some groups and individuals assuredly see themselves as residing in paradise and being immune to corruption and temptations of power and wealth, just because they have the knowledge of religious rules, perform the obligatory acts, and avoid forbidden acts as dictated by Islamic jurisprudential rules. They thus consider themselves above scrutiny and accountability to the public. For them, it is the masses instead who are prone to corruption and perdition. Accordingly, they believe that government-appointed religious and other officials are obliged to prevent the masses from corruption by enjoining right and forbidding wrong to them.

In fact, however, the opposite of the above mechanism is true. Rulers resemble citizens by nature. "Power tends to corrupt and absolute power corrupts absolutely" (Acton, 1887). There is a direct relationship between the degree of influence of corruption on the destiny of society and the degree of power and influence of individuals and social institutions. Therefore, state corruption is the gravest wrong that should be fought against, and politicians need to be publicly monitored and checked more than anyone else in society. This is thematically featured in the Islamic narrations about en-joining right and forbidding wrong. For example, some nar-rations refer to the fact that the abandonment of enjoining right and forbidding wrong renders prayers ineffective and leads to the domination of wrongdoers over society (Ku-leyni, 1986: p. 374).

It can be said that the worst wrong that Imam Hussein encountered at the time was a corrupt political state or ca-liphate being run in the name of Islam. He said, "I have not risen but to seek reform in the nation of my grandfather" (Majlisi, 1982: 44/329). He did not say that the masses were corrupt, or that he should take power to reform the mass of Muslims. In fact, history shows that, essentially, the reform of the masses in this way not only seems impractical but also that it returns the opposite effect. The *ummah*, or Islamic society, in Imam Hussein's quotation cited above, is not the *subject* but the *locus* of reform. In fact, the subject of reform is the dictatorial political system, which sees itself as the ca-liph of Prophet Muhammad and the representative of God on earth, in charge of the worldly and otherworldly affairs of the ummah. The dictatorial political system can only be reformed through monitoring of rulers and politicians by the civil society. It seems clear that Imam Hussein tried to establish a just state based on meta-religious morality, which was also part of the mission of Prophet Muhammad. Howev-er, as the Qur'ān (57/25) reiterates, The main responsibility in this case is delegated to people (Qur'ān 57/25), and the Prophet and Imam can undertake the responsibility when-ever people's request gives the final reason to do so (Radhi, 1993: Sermon 3).

3.11. Moṭahhari's Jurisprudential (fiqhi) Explanation

Moṭahhari also offered a third explanation about the Battle of Karbala. He believes that there were three factors at work in Imam Hussein's uprising: (1) rejecting Yazīd's call for allegiance, (2) positively responding to the invitation of the people of Kufa and establish his case against them, and (3) enjoining the right and forbidding the wrong. Moṭahhari considers this third factor as the main one, with the other two being complementary to it. He thus argues that even in the absence of complementary factors, Imam Hussein would have revolted because of his duty of enjoining right and forbidding wrong (1998: pp. 134–149).

This explanation by Moṭahhari has some merits. For instance, unlike other explications, it does not presuppose that Imam Hussein was motivated only by a single factor. Despite this merit, Moṭahhari's explanation can be criticised in several respects.

First, it is not profound enough, because it does not tell us why Imam Hussein did not acquiesce to taking an oath of allegiance to Yazīd. We know that Imam ʿAli eventually gave an oath of allegiance to Abu Bakr, Omar, and Osman, and that most Imams that followed him paid their allegiance to the tyrannical ruler of the time. Does Imam Hussein's different approach from them all lie in the difference between Yazīd and the other unjust rulers? It seems that there is a greater difference at work which has something to do with the transformations of the political structures and the institutions of state.

Second, concerning the criticism of the theory of *Shahīd-e Javid*, Moṭahhari agrees with Sharīʿatī, that Imam Hussein's

main motivation was not to accept the invitation of the Kufians and establish an Islamic state: "It is clear that Imam Hussein, right from the beginning of his movement, knew that
the Kufians were not ready, that they were weak-minded and
subdued" (Moṭahhari, 1998: p. 143). On the other hand, he
posits: "How would history judge Imam Hussein? Definitely,
if he had ignored the Kufians, we now would certainly ask,
why did he not accept their invitation?" (*ibid.*); and later that
"Imam Hussein here faces a historical dilemma; if he does
not respond to the request of the Kufians, he is certainly held
responsible. It will be judged that the circumstances looked
extremely favourable, but Imam Hussein could not or did
not grasp the opportunity or he was afraid to do so – and
similar judgements. To prove his case against the people who
had asked his succour, Imam Hussein responded to their request as described before" (*ibid.*: p. 319).

However, Moṭahhari's claim poses a paradox. If Imam
Hussein had already known that the revolt against the
Umayyads would fail partially or completely, he could have
given the justification that his uprising would be in vain in
those circumstances – leaving aside the fact that what was
paramount for him was to gain divine satisfaction and a sa-
tiated conscience, without care for the judgements and rep-
rimands of history.

Moreover, Moṭahhari somehow mixes the "Imam's establishing his case against people" with "people's establishing their case against the Imam". That people declare their
readiness to cooperate with the Imam completes the proof
upon the Imam to embark on an uprising. However, if the
Imam knows beforehand that people are dishonest, unloy-

al and unreliable, the mere declaration of readiness is not considered as completion of the proof upon Imam. In this case, the Imam is no longer responsible for an uprising. In addition, relying on the evidence indicating that the Kufians were weak-minded and prone to be disloyal, Imam Hussein could have rejected their request, and then it would not have been necessary for him to go as far as martyrdom to complete the proof upon them.

Another problem with Moṭahhari's theory is that apparently, he tries to provide a purely jurisprudential justification for the Imam's movement due to the incorrect assumption he holds regarding the exclusivity of Sharī'a as the unique source of values and norms for the Imam's actions. That is, his perspective on allegiance, responding to the invitation of the people of Kufa, and enjoining right and forbidding wrong is purely jurisprudential. However, it is very difficult to justify Imam Hussein's movement to Shi'as, let alone Sunnis, especially the Imam's opponents as well as non-Muslims, with a jurisprudential understanding these reasons for action. This is because enjoining right and forbidding wrong has certain conditions from a jurisprudential standpoint, some of which are missing in this case. One of those conditions is the likelihood of influence, while Yazīd and his entourage and representatives were not the kind of people who would be moved by the Imam's protest. The second condition for the religious obligation of enjoining right and forbidding wrong from a jurisprudential perspective is that it should not involve considerable danger or harm, and the greatest harm is death.

One might argue, however, that the condition is applicable only to the cases where the very foundation of Islam is not at risk. At the time, the Imam considered it was because the caliph was a dog-fancier, monkey-fancier, a wine consumer, and incestuous. However, these are by no means persuasive cases because Mu'awiya was even more dangerous to Islam than Yazīd; and if Islam's being at risk had been the very basis of Imam Hussein's movement, then in principle, he could have revolted during the reign of Mu'awiya. There is also the question as to how the uprising that would knowingly fail could avert the danger posed to Islam. Avoidance to pay an oath of allegiance and respond positively to the invitation of the Kufians cannot be easily explained on the basis of Islamic jurisprudence (*fiqh*). This series of errors and criticisms makes it understandable why the Shi'a commonly accept the view that Imam Hussein's movement was either a hidden secret or based on an exclusive command from God that remains unexplainable by universal Shar'ia-based rules.

Another problem that arises from the fact that the decisions Imam Hussein made and acted accordingly – following his knowledge of martyrdom of Muslim ibn 'Aqeel and reluctance of the Kufians – cannot be reasonably explained on the basis of enjoining right and forbidding wrong. Moreover, this theory is not compatible with some historical data. For instance, under the siege of ibn Ziyad's Kufian infantry, Imam Hussein said to the Kufians, "I came here at your invitation. Now that you have withdrawn your invitation, go about your business, and I will return to Medina" (ibn Ṭawus, 1969: pp. 77–78). Here the Imam meant that from now on, I no longer have sufficient justification for uprising, and the duty I had until now has been lifted from my shoulders due to your breach of covenant. He did not mean that you should go about your business while I leave and rise up again elsewhere. Imam Hussein was neither the kind of person to make such an unreasonable request, nor would his enemies have accepted it.

3.12. Pros and Cons of the Proposed Explanations

The three above explanations share three positive points. First, they explain Imam Hussein's movement as being based on rationality, ordinary human reason, and the evaluation of information obtained from the ordinary (as opposed to divine) sources of knowledge that were available to the people in general. Second, Imam Hussein is seen as being motivated by a sense of duty. Third, the motive underlying his uprising was the universal duty rather than an exclusive duty based on divine command. Therefore, later generations who might face similar circumstances are able to emulate him.

In other words, these explanations have three notable characteristics. First, they are natural, and humanistic explanations. Second, they are considered axiological and normative. Trying to explore and describe the reasons underlying Imam Hussein's behaviour, they presuppose that the Imam followed specific norms and values. Third, the putative values or norms are universal and not specific to the Imam himself, hence, generalisable at least to all Muslims, if not all of humanity.

To put it more clearly, the underlying assumption of all these explanations, which is indeed a correct assumption, is that a free and autonomous agent needs a reason for their voluntary action that both *justifies* that action and *motivates* them to perform it. If we assume that Imam Hussein's movement was a voluntary action, we must accept that Imam Hussein, with complete freedom and autonomy, evaluated the various options and possibilities available to him, consulted with like-minded wise people and compassionate advisors, and gathered all information that could be obtained through ordinary sources of knowledge; and then combined this information with his accepted values, made a decision, and acted according to that decision. Therefore, we must accept that Imam Hussein had rational reason(s) for his actions that both justified this course for him and motivated him to act.

Yet these explanations suffer from a major problem in that they try to interpret Imam Hussein's justification for his action either as merely based on religious, Shari'a-related, and Islamic jurisprudential grounds (according to Moṭahhari and Sharī'atī)[14], or as being based on religious and Sharī'a-related grounds along with the legal basis (according to Najafābādī). However, as already explained before, the justification based on which Imam Hussein acted seems to be moral, meta-religious, meta-jurisprudential, and meta-legal, for the duties of fighting against the oppressor, enjoining right and forbidding wrong, and avoiding the oath of allegiance in those circumstances are all moral duties recognised by Islam. Therefore, it can be claimed that Imam Hussein is an exemplar and model not only for Muslims and Shi'a but also for all humans since morality is essentially a meta-religious category.

---

[14] Referring to martyrdom as a religious duty like prayers, fasting, hajj, zakat, and jihad, Sharī'atī believes that Imam Hussein's duty in those specific circumstances was martyrdom. Yet he considers martyrdom not as an individual duty but of every Muslim who finds themselves in the same situation as the Imam's (see Sharī'atī, 1988: pp. 125–195 and pp. 211–225).

Imam Hussein somewhere said to the enemy army, "If you do not have any religion, then at least be free in your present life." This exactly means that not only is the enemy's conduct wrong and condemned according to the religious reasons but also it is wrong and unjustifiable in line with the meta-religious reasons. Therefore, to avoid the misbehaviours does not require being a Muslim or a Shiʿa, but being a human being would suffice. Such a line of argument would be acceptable and reasonable if we presupposed moral criteria that are universal and rooted in the very human identity and nature. What those justifications were the topic to be dealt with in the next session.

CHAPTER FOUR

Imam Hussein: The School of Justice and Dignity

4.1. Introduction

In Chapter 3, we examined several explanations offered for the Battle of Karbala. For a historical event to carry meaningful lessons, we must first gain a correct understanding through analysing the intentions of the agents who engaged in it. This requires examining relevant historical reports to formulate an explanation more plausible than alternatives. Superior explanations are not only compatible with evidence but also demonstrate coherence and alignment with valid background assumptions.

A metaphysical or mythical explanation of historical events, even if true, provides limited practical guidance for human conduct, if any. By emphasising divine intervention or unseen factors while diminishing human agency, such explanations offer no valuable lessons to follow. In contrast, explanations with practical benefit emphasise the role of human agency within its historical context.

Having critically examined five different explanations previously, we will now discuss another approach that appears more plausible. Before proceeding, however, three points warrant consideration:

1. The list of explanations that were reviewed here is not exhaustive. There are other explanations related to the Battle of Karbala that are available or can be obtained, and an examination of all of them is beyond the scope

of our session.

2. Just as Imam Hussein and his companions made their decisions and actions based on some reason(s), so did Yazīd and his army. Since this event was the product of the interaction between two groups, a comprehensive explanation of it requires discovering both groups' reasons for their actions. However, due to time constraints, we are forced to postpone the examination of the principles governing the mindset of Yazīd and his followers to another time. Here, I will discuss only two normative principles that governed the behaviour of the Umayyad dynasty, which are not limited to their political and moral philosophy, but rather common among all autocrats: 'the necessity of preserving government at any cost' and 'victory through terror'.

3. In addition to the type of explanation that we are looking for, the breadth of its inclusion is also of particular importance here. If the reasons governing Imam Hussein's decision-making are unique to the Shi'a belief and value system, then he should only be a role model for the Shi'a. In addition, if these reasons were based on specific Islamic (intra-religious) system of beliefs and values, non-Muslims will not be able to look at the Imam as a role model either. However, if the reasons governing the Imam's behaviour are not restricted to any specific religious or sectarian system of beliefs and values, then all human beings will be able to look at the Imam as a role model.

As far as I know, among those who have tried to explain the

event of Karbala, Ṣāliḥī Najafābādī is the only one who has
paid attention to the last point. In describing his approach to
writing *Shahid-e Javid* [*The Eternal Martyr*], he writes:

> Since Hussein ibn Ali (as) is a global figure, our discussion in
> this book is carried out on a global level. Therefore, we have
> examined the issues related to the Imam's uprising from a
> wider perspective than the Shi'a world's, through natural
> means, rational paths ways and legal principles, so that it can
> also be understood and accepted by non-Shi'a readers as well.
> (Najafābādī 1970: p.6)

The terms "natural means" and "rational paths" in the above
quote refer to the Imam's process of decision-making, but
"legal principles" refer to the normative foundations that justify his decisions. In order for a process of decision-making
to be understandable and acceptable to all humans, it must
rely on the natural reasons for action and universal norms of
practical rationality that all humans tend to share. However,
since the validity of legal principles depends on their recognition by all humans, and these principles evolve over time
and place, we cannot generalise them to include all humans.
Therefore, the only viable alternative that can have such a
function is the universal principles of morality.

4.2. Two Rival Theories in Political Philosophy

In the Umayyad conception of Islam, political power is an
end in itself which has *intrinsic* value and justifies any means
necessary to attain and maintain it. According to this politi-

cal theory, when it comes to attaining or maintaining political power, anything is permissible. The ruler is the master, and the people are his slaves; the arbitrary will of the master is the source of his slaves' rights and duties. The answer to the question "How should one govern?" is not predetermined, but rather depends on the arbitrary will of the ruler. The right to absolute rule means that it is not bound by any moral or religious restrictions; rather, religious and moral norms and values are whatever the ruler decrees.

On the other hand, according to the 'Alawīte conception of Islam, political power is not an end in itself, and hence does not have *intrinsic* value. Rather, it is just a means, and therefore, its value is *extrinsic*. In political domain, justice is the aim. Other things, including political power, are valuable only to the extent that they are means towards the realisation of justice. Therefore, if preserving political power involves oppression, it will have no value, and becomes immoral.

In a story recounted by ibn Abbas in *Nahj al-Balāghah*, he says:

> During the Battle of Jamal, I went to Imam 'Ali's tent and saw him repairing his shoes. The Imam asked me, "What is the value of this shoe sole?" I replied, "Nothing." The Imam said, "I swear to God, the value of ruling over you in my eyes is less than that of this shoe sole, unless through it I can establish a right and eliminate a wrong."

Here, "establishing right" means realising justice. Therefore, in 'Alawīte political philosophy, justice is the foremost virtue, not political power; and the latter becomes valuable only in light of the former, not vice versa. Political power is merely a tool that is worthless in itself, and only has value as long as it can be used to build a just society and take the right of the oppressed back from the oppressor. In contrast, in Umayyad political philosophy, power has intrinsic value and is desirable in and of itself; and preserving it at any cost, even at the cost of oppression, is considered obligatory.

Contrastingly, if you look at the history of Karbala, you will observe that many of the atrocities and savage acts that the Yazīd's army meted out were overmeasure, especially those that were committed in the aftermath of Imam Hussein and his companions' martyrdom, such as running horses over the bodies of the martyrs, raising their severed heads on spears, taking their women and children captive, and marching them around the towns and cities enroute Damascus. These crimes cannot be justified except by someone who acts out of conviction in the principle of "victory through terror". Yazīd and his army wanted to terrorise others in this way and practically convey to people that when we do this to the Prophet's grandson and his family, others should know that they will neither be spared.

Yet more principles can be recounted to explain the political philosophy of the Umayyad dynasty, such as it would seem, "might makes right". This, however, requires much further discussion for another occasion. In any case, Karbala is regarded as the scene of a confrontation between two incompatible political philosophies, which have a long history that pre-dates Islam, and are based on two incompatible versions of political morality.

In summary, it can be said that here we are dealing with

a theory in political ethics that can be labelled as the "ruler's command theory of ethics". This is in fact regarded as an adaptation of the "divine command theory" in the realm of politics, whereby the ruler takes the place of God, and ethical values originate from His command.

4.3. The Moral Explanation of the Battle of Karbala

Let us now turn to the moral reasons by which Imam Hussein justified his movement. In general, it can be said that the Battle of Karbala was caused by the separation of religion from morality. If religion goes beyond its moral framework, and if the religious government violates moral principles in the name of God, then it can be said that an evil has prevailed in society that must be fought against and, if necessary, be martyred for.

It seems that this is the biggest and most dangerous corruption that a religious community can face. Such viciousness not only destroys people's lives, but also their religion and salvation. Of course, such corruption can also be found in non-religious societies, but the difference is that when it appears in a religious community, it takes place in the name of God and is justified by providing religious reasons.

What did Yazīd's soldiers claim? And what justification did they have for their barbaric behaviour? Their argument was that Yazīd was the successor of the Messenger of God, and that it was a religious duty of all Muslims to obey his orders without question. In other words, opposition of Yazīd was viewed as tantamount to being the opposition of the Messenger of God, and thus, as defiance of God too. Consequently, in the minds of Yazīd's soldiers, those who chose not to pledge allegiance to him and instead rebelled against him, were deemed apostates and that they should therefore, face severe consequences.

The justification that Imam Hussein had for his stance was not that if he were in place of Yazīd, rulership for him was permissible in the same way as it was being deemed for Yazīd. There are people who refer to Yazīd's habits and behaviours, such as playing with dogs and monkeys, as the justification for Imam Hussein's movement. They ignore the difference between Yazīd's method of governance and that of the Prophet and Imam ʿAli; and thus, unjustly compare Imam Hussein with Yazīd. Ironically, the latter himself acknowledged that making such comparison was out of order.

Yazīd's claim was that God had willed for him to rule over people as the caliph of the Messenger of God with the same personal qualities, lineage, behaviour, and governance policy that the Imam had. He used to say: "My legitimacy is from God, and my rule is endorsed by God. Therefore, my will is divine will and opposition to me is opposition of God." Imam Hussein rejected this. If he did not, the extinction of true Islam, namely ʿAlawīte Islam, would be inevitable. In other words, what would have remained was Umayyad Islam, which in essence would have been the reviving of polytheism and injustice of the *Jāhiliyyah* period pretending to be Islam.

Imam Hussein articulated his aspirations for this movement through his speeches. He explicitly outlined his objectives in a will that he composed prior to departing Medina, entrusting it to his brother, Muhammad ibn al-Ḥanafīyah, to ensure its preservation in history. Within this will, the Imam initially affirmed his belief in the unity of God and the prophecy of Prophet Muhammad. This was likely done for two reasons: first, to anticipate and counteract potential accusations of apostasy and hostility towards the Prophet that could have been perpetrated by the influential Umayyad propaganda machinery; and second, he anticipated being raised to a divine status by some of his ignorant followers.

Next, the Imam says:

> I did not rise up in vain, nor did I rise up for the sake of mischief, corruption or oppression. Rather, I rose up to seek reformation in my grandfather's nation. I want to enjoin right and forbid wrong and follow the path of my grandfather and father. (Majlisi 1982: 329/44)

As I mentioned in the previous chapter, "my grandfather's nation" here is the context for the reforms that Imam Hussein sought, not the subject. The clause "I follow the path of my grandfather and father" is an explanatory reference to the preceding clause "I want to enjoin right and forbid wrong". This clause shows that Imam Hussein's aim of promoting virtue and preventing vice was related to the prevalent method of corrupt and deviant governance in the Islamic society. Yazīd's governance had no compatibility with that of Prophet Muhammad and Imam ʿAli. The latter two did not seek autocracy, and only pursued justice. Yazīd, on the other hand, wanted power for the sake of power and considered justice subordinate to his own will and command. He attributed such a view of political philosophy to God, and the Prophet erroneously.

This was the greatest wrong that Imam Hussein had to rise up against as his moral and religious obligation. The wrong was the oppression of people, not the Caliph's playing with dogs and monkeys. Additionally, following the footsteps of his father, Imam 'Ali, Imam Hussein's goal was not to seize power, as vindicated by his reference to Imam 'Ali's saying: "Oh God, you know that our goal is not competition for power" (ibn Shu'bah al-Ḥarranī, 1984: p. 239). Imam Hussein's further aim was to change political structures and institutions, not individuals, because changing individuals will not cure any societal ills unless it led to transforming governance structures and institutions. By implementing reforms to *structures* and *institutions*, the likelihood of individuals abusing their power significantly diminishes; and if abuse does occur, it becomes easier to swiftly dismiss those responsible for it.

4.4. The Place of Justice and Human Dignity Among Moral Values

Justice and dignity hold a unique place among moral values; they serve as the foundation and inspiration for the other values. As I see it, an insightful examination of Imam Hussein's speeches and actions reveals that he consistently upheld and exemplified these two profound moral values throughout his movement. During the final year of his life, following the demise of Mu'awiya and the ascension of Yazīd, Imam Hussein made two crucial decisions that were rooted in both justice and dignity. It is important to note that his uprising was not a blind movement based on some irrational emotions, or blind obedience to a divine private command, but rather followed universal rational and moral reasons that he had carefully examined.

The first decision made by Imam Hussein, which led to his departure from Medina, was to confront the oppressive and tyrannical rule of Yazīd and strive for the establishment of a just government with the support of the Kufans. This course of action is based solely on the grounds of justice, which stands as the foremost value in social and political morality. Up until that point, the Imam's actions were guided by Imam ʿAli's principle: "Stand with the oppressed and challenge the oppressor" (Sayyid Raḍī, 1993: Letter 47).

The second fateful decision that Imam Hussein made was the one he took midway through his journey, after learning about the martyrdom of Muslim ibn ʿAqīl and the desertion of the people of Kufa, and he acted according to this decision until the end of the Battle of Karbala. When faced with the enemy's ultimatum to either surrender and pledge allegiance or face death, he chose to embrace death with dignity rather than live in humiliation. At this stage, the moral principle guiding the Imam's actions was, "We shall not succumb to disgrace" (Ṭabarsi 1982: 300/2). This decision and corresponding action can only be justified based on the value of human dignity and the moral duty to uphold it.

4.5. How to Strive for Social Justice

The principle of justice emphasises our moral responsibility to combat injustice and actively work towards achieving justice. However, it is important to acknowledge that addressing pervasive social injustice and striving for social justice on a larger scale necessitate moral considerations regarding certain conditions and stages. Injustice manifests in diverse forms, all of which contribute to the deprivation or neglect of rights. In any situation where injustice arises, it is crucial for justice to prevail over those who perpetrate it, regardless of whether they are individuals, groups or governments, because they disregard or violate fundamental rights of the oppressed. Therefore, if there is no respect of rights, there will be no injustice.

When Imam Hussein says, "I want to follow the path of my grandfather and father", he also means that he has not risen up for his personal rights. This is a part of Imam 'Ali's way of living. When people, or the six-member council appointed by Umar, decided to pledge allegiance to Uthman as the third caliph, Imam 'Ali said, "Certainly you know that I deserve this position (caliphate) more than anyone else. By God, I will submit (to the new caliph) so long as the affairs of Muslims are secured and there is no injustice against [anyone] except me alone. I do this to seek reward and excellence (from God) and because I have no interest in the vanities and luxuries (of this world) that you compete for" (Raḍī, 1993: Sermon 74).

"Justice", as Rawls (1999: p. 3) states, "is the first virtue of social institutions, as truth is of systems of thought."[15] Within

---

[15] The full paragraph containing the quote is: "Justice is the first virtue of social institutions, as truth is of systems of thought. A theory however elegant and economical must be rejected or revised if it is untrue; likewise, laws and institutions no matter how efficient and well-arranged must be reformed or abolished if they are unjust. Each person possesses an inviolability founded on justice that even the welfare of society as a whole cannot override. For this reason, justice denies that the loss of freedom for some is made right by a greater good shared by others. It does not allow that the sacrifices imposed on a few are outweighed by the larger sum of advantages enjoyed by many. Therefore, in a just society the liberties of

a truly just society, social institutions are established on the basis of individual rights and operated in accordance with these rights. When engaging with individuals, these institutions uphold and safeguard their rights without infringement. It is vital to note that social justice encompasses more than just economic equity; it also encompasses political justice. Political justice entails the equitable allocation of power, responsibility, freedom and other available communal resources and public goods among all citizens.

Therefore, freedom and justice are not mutually exclusive. That is, human beings are not compelled to make a choice between justice and freedom, sacrificing one for the sake of the other. Instead, justice serves as a standard by which the allocation of freedom and other public goods should be conducted. When freedoms are withheld or unevenly distributed, it exemplifies an act of injustice. The public sphere represents a shared domain for citizens, wherein everyone possesses an equal stake. If an ruler seizes control of this sphere without the presence of the public or their duly elected representatives and without their consent, such occupation becomes invasive and unjust. Consequently, it becomes the moral responsibility of the people to combat and resist such injustices.

However, as I previously mentioned, this duty has conditions, prerequisites and stages that must be observed. The initial step in addressing social injustice is engaging in social activism. During this phase, those who are aware of such oppression within society have a moral obligation to raise

---

equal citizenship are taken as settled; the rights secured by justice are not subject to political bargaining or to the calculus of social interests."

awareness among their fellow citizens regarding the presence of this oppression and call everyone's attention to this collective moral duty. At this stage, individual rebellion and uprising against injustice, especially armed ones, are improper and unwise acts. Social activism for political reforms is a collective duty, although the responsibility of elites, scholars and thinkers is greater in this regard. The goal of social activism is to sensitise the public conscience about injustice.

The social activism that is devoted to achieving political justice includes theorising about justice, because without a clear and well-developed theory of justice, it is impossible to identify instances of injustice or work towards achieving justice. Theories serve as guides for action, and those who act without a well-considered, defensible, and executable theory do not make progress; in fact, their actions may cause more harm than good. Just society cannot be established through slogans alone; many people who have risen up against the existing situation with the slogan of justice have only succeeded in returning society to its previous state from which people were already trying to be liberated.

Human history has demonstrated that the displacement of individuals in an oppressive society does not necessarily transform it into a just society, nor does it replace unjust structures and institutions with equitable ones. This is one of the key differences between a revolution and reform. Revolutionary movements are focused on the displacement of individuals and often remain limited to this extent. Revolutionaries mistakenly believe that certain individuals who hold positions of power are the main cause of social corruptions, and by removing or eliminating those individuals, the problem would be resolved. They reduce the sociology of power and political corruption to the psychology of power and political corruption.

However, social problems have social roots and are nourished by social structures. Therefore, as long as the social structure is not reformed, the displacement of individuals will not alleviate the ordinary people's difficulties. Rather, after a while, the same previous relations will be re-established under new titles and in new clothing, and new individuals who come to power cannot stop or change this trend, regardless of their initial intentions. Instead, the corrupt and unjust structure will change their personality, character, mindset, and behaviour.

Social justice, which is the primary virtue of social institutions, differs from individual justice, which is the virtue of individuals. These two justices should not be considered identical, or one being subsumed under the other. Achieving social justice is impossible without collective participation and without citizens' awareness and sensitivity towards the oppressive structure and its role in the emergence and continuation of the current situation.

In other words, social oppression has social origins, and it should not be reduced to the psychology of oppressive rulers. The unjust structures and institutions of political power, which are social entities, are so powerful and influential that they change the temperament and personality of the power holders in their own favour. Therefore, in this context psychology follows sociology, not the other way around.

Individual justice of the rulers cannot replace an oppressive structure and institution with a just one. Instead, oppressive structures and institutions will turn an individual who was just before they came to power into a tyrannical ruler, while just structures and institutions control and restrain individual oppression and prevent its emergence, influential and institutionalisation. There is a difference between when a tyrant individual reaches power in a just structure and when a just individual reaches power in an oppressive structure. Pharaonic structures and institutions make the pharaoh, not the other way around.

After individuals become aware and conscious, and their collective conscience becomes sensitive, it may be time for peaceful social struggles. Entering this stage requires two important conditions. The first condition is the readiness of citizens in sufficient numbers. If the number of people willing to participate in a collective struggle against social injustice is insufficient, the responsibility of peaceful social struggle will be lifted from the intellectual leaders. Their duty will be limited only to social activism aimed at raising awareness and correcting citizens' understanding of the source of the problem and its solution. This is because on the one hand, ought implies can, and on the other hand, social struggles are focused on results, and the desired outcome of this struggle can only be achieved if a sufficient number of citizens are willing to participate in this struggle to the necessary extent and pay the necessary cost.

The second condition for entering this stage pertains to the *method* of struggle. In this stage, one must only use peaceful methods, tools, and strategies, such as civil disobedience, because if the goal can be achieved through peaceful means without resorting to force and violence, then resorting to these will be morally unjustifiable. Violence and the use of force are always the last resort and should only be used when all other options have been exhausted.

Political injustice is a social disease, and if it can be fought peacefully, violence and force should not be used. If an oppressive and tyrannical government submits peacefully to the demands of justice seekers, they do not have the moral right and are barred from resorting to force. For this reason, when God orders Moses and his brother Aaron to go and fight Pharaoh, who had become defiant, He tells them: "Go to Pharaoh. Indeed, he has transgressed. And say to him a gentle word. Perhaps he may remember or fear [God]" (Qur'ān 20: 43–44). This means that they should speak gently with Pharaoh, perhaps he will be reminded and have an awakening to refrain from wrongdoing towards his people and arrogance towards God.

Later, I will talk about the application of this important moral principle on the movement of Imam Hussein, and we will see what significant results considering this principle bear upon our current duties. Imam Hussein never sought violence and throughout his journey and parleys with the enemy until the last moment of his life, he had tried to prevent a battle from enfolding. Nevertheless, a war of attrition was imposed on him. Of course, digesting this statement may be difficult for some, but the truth is so clear in his behaviour and words that denying it is denying the obvious.

In modern political culture, this type of struggle is called "civil disobedience". It means expressing opposition to an unjust law or government without resorting to violence. It is actually rooted in human rights. Imam Hussein's actions can also be considered a form of civil disobedience until he realised that the people of Kufa had broken their promise and were not willing to support him. The justification that Imam Hussein had for his struggle was that the people of Kufa had invited him to come to them and help reform the political structure of the community, and it was both his and their right to do so.

However, if a tyrannical government resists the legitimate demands of the people and refuses to relinquish its tyranny without resorting to force, and does not reform its unjust laws and structures, nor allow others to do so, then the people have the right to resort to force within the moral framework in order to achieve justice. This is the third stage in the struggle against tyranny and the quest for political justice. However, this stage also has conditions, and one of these is that citizens must be willing to cooperate and make sacrifice; and if there is an insufficient number of individuals, the leaders of social struggles are absolved of their obligation to undertake this type of jihad.

Therefore, Imam Hussein changed his line of argument after he became aware that Muslim ibn 'Aqīl was killed, and that the people of Kufa had betrayed him. In various cases, both in public speeches and private negotiations with Yazīd's soldiers who were mostly from Kufa, the Imam said to them, "O people of Kufa, you invited me to come to you. Now that you have withdrawn your invitation, leave me to my fate and resume your daily lives, while I return to Medina or go somewhere else and live with my life." (ibn 'Abbas had suggested that he goes to Yemen). However, the Yazīdis said, "We will not leave you alone. Either you must pledge allegiance to Yazīd or be killed" (ibn Ṭāwūs, 1969: pp. 77–78). As I mentioned, the decision Imam Hussein made at this juncture and the opposition he endured until the last drop of his blood was spilled is justified under the principle of human dignity, and the moral imperative of preserving this dignity.

4.6. Human Dignity and its Place in Morality

According to some moral philosophers, like Kant, human dignity is the foundation of ethics. In simpler terms, "human dignity" as a normative concept means that human beings are persons, not objects. Therefore, they should not be treated as mere tools. To treat a person as an object is to violate their human dignity. For example, cheating in elections and disregarding citizens' votes, deceiving or manipulating them, or engineering elections are not only immoral for other reasons, but also immoral because these misconducts violate the human dignity of those affected. The principle of human dignity requires us to view ourselves and others as ends in themselves, not merely means to an end. Morality demands that we respect human dignity in ourselves and others and do not violate it, nor allow others to do so.

Human dignity is both the foundation of human rights and the source of human responsibilities. In one sense, all the rights that human beings possess and all the duties that they owe to themselves and others, stem from their human dignity in one way or another. Dignity is a special moral status of human beings and the distinguishing feature of humans from animate and inanimate objects. We have the right to treat an object like a tool. That is, to own it, buy and sell it, and use it for our own benefit. However, it is impermissible to treat ourselves and other humans in this way.

Islamic ethics emphasises upon the importance of human dignity. Both the Qur'ān and Hadiths instruct us not to sell ourselves for anything less than paradise (Raḍī, 1993: saying 456), which is nothing but the moral virtues we cultivate within ourselves and the personality that encompasses these virtues. We have an inner paradise and an outer paradise; the latter is actually a manifestation and reflection of the former. The Ahlul-Bayt state that "God has entrusted everything to the believer except for humiliating oneself" (Kulayni, 1986: p. 63-5), and also "the most intelligent people are those who distance themselves from this world" (Amodi, 1989: p. 197). The principle of dignity states that human value is greater than the world and its possessions, and therefore, someone who respects their human dignity and understands its worth will not trade or bargain it with anything worldly. Someone who can be bought with money or position or other things, and someone who remains silent in the face of injustice due to fear or greed, and submits to humiliation and subjugation, does not know their own worth and thus, cheaply sells themselves.

4.7. Human Dignity in the Battle of Karbala

The principle of dignity states that human life only has value and significance if it is accompanied by dignity, and a person does not have the right to disregard it or allow others to trample it in exchange for life. In other words, if we are forced to choose between life with humiliation and death with honour, the principle of dignity dictates that we should choose the latter. This was the situation that Imam Hussein was faced with in Karbala – and he was indeed confronted with a significant choice. If the Yazīdis did not force him to pledge allegiance to their caliph, his human dignity would not have been placed in a state of compromise, and from a moral standpoint, he would not have become obligated to choose death over life.

What the Imam did here was not a rebellion or a fight, but an act of self-defence: one of human dignity, which as stated before, is a fundamental right that every individual possesses. Going forward, discussions of the Imam's "rebellion" or uprising ceased as the people of Kufa had distanced themselves, relieving the Imam of any moral obligation to initiate a revolt. If the Yazīdis had refrained from pressuring him for allegiance, he would have peacefully pursued his personal interests, engaged in social activism that enlightened the masses.

If the Imam had been let go, his act of fighting would have been morally unjustifiable. War should be regarded as a last resort rather than a goal, because its value lies solely in its ability to achieve a legitimate objective – such as the attainment of social justice and the establishment of a just government. However, considering the opposition of the people of Kufa towards such a goal, it is evident that its realisation was unattainable.

Further, it is important to note that martyrdom is not a goal within Islamic teachings; instead, it is viewed as a means. This is due to the immense value placed upon human life, allowing sacrifice only when something of greater significance is at stake, making it necessary to preserve it.

Thus, in summary, sacrificing oneself is deemed morally impermissible in two instances. First, when sacrificing oneself for matters that possess moral worth lower than the preservation of human life; second, when sacrificing oneself for matters that hold moral significance greater than human life, when it remains feasible to safeguard these more valuable things by alternative methods, incurring lesser costs and sacrificing less significant aspects.

4.8. Moral Explanation of the Battle of Karbala

In this regard, as stated previously, Imam Hussein's school imparts two crucial moral lessons: the first pertains to the importance of combating oppression and advocating for political justice, while the second insists upon the significance of respecting human dignity. Prior to receiving news of Muslim ibn ʿAqīl's martyrdom and the abandonment of the people of Kufa, Imam Hussein's moral obligation was to actively resist the Umayyad regime's oppressive rule and strive to rectify its unjust systems and institutions. However, following these events and the subsequent shift in circumstances, Imam Hussein's moral obligation changed, placing a new responsibility on his shoulders: the preservation of his own human dignity. Consequently, every aspect of Imam Hussein's movement, from its inception to its conclusion, was grounded in moral principles and supported by rational reasoning. His conduct remained fully aligned with moral values throughout, making him an exemplary role model for all of humanity, regardless of their religious affiliations or beliefs.

Imam Hussein declares, "There is a [good] exemplar for you in me" (al-Kufi, 1996: p. 172). The Imam's intent is that we can learn from him how to live and how to die. Furthermore, he clarifies why he embarked on the journey towards Mecca and Kufa, asserting:

> I did not rise up in vain, nor did I rise up for the sake of mischief, corruption or oppression. Rather, I rose up to seek reformation in the ummah of my grandfather. I want to enjoin right and forbid wrong and follow the path of my grandfather and father. (Majlisi, 1982: vol. 44, p. 329)

By integrating the teachings of Imam Hussein and Imam 'Ali[16] on the significance of justice and the duty of humanity in combating oppression, it becomes evident that Imam Hussein initiated his movement from Medina with the aim of opposing oppression and establishing political justice. Nevertheless, in Karbala, the rallying cry of this revered figure was: "We shall not succumb to disgrace" (Ṭabarsi, 1982: vol. 2, p. 300). This declaration highlights the Imam's moral commitment to safeguarding human dignity and refusal to submit to humiliation. These two moral obligations extend universally to all human beings, demonstrating that Imam Hussein's move-

---

[16] For example: "Be an adversary to the oppressor and a supporter to the oppressed" (*Nahj al-Balāghah*, Letter 47). Also this: "Behold, by Him who split the grain (to grow) and created living beings, if people had not come to me and supporters had not exhausted the argument and if there had been no pledge of Allah with the learned to the effect that they should not acquiesce in the gluttony of the oppressor and the hunger of the oppressed, I would have cast the rope of caliphate on its own shoulders, and would have given the last one the same treatment as to the first one. Then you would have seen that in my view this world of yours is no better than the sneezing of a goat." (*Nahj al-Balāghah*, Sermon 3).

ment was not founded solely on a personal divine directive that excluded others, nor was it based solely on legal and religious or sectarian justifications that pertain predominantly to Shi'as and Muslims.

Imam Hussein represents a valuable school, teaching us important lessons about courage, freedom, and resistance against oppression. However, it is regrettable that the Shi'as often limit themselves to mourning him instead of truly learning from his teachings. Mere mourning, devoid of insight, does not contribute to achieving the ideals for which he made the ultimate sacrifice. Imam Hussein did not become a martyr solely for the purpose of being mourned; his sacrifice aims to gain an eternal life (Qur'ān 3: 169-171) and guide us in living and making decisions according to certain values and principles. Sadly, our way of life does not always reflect Imam Hussein as our role model, as we sometimes succumb to moral hypocrisy. By remaining silent in the face of oppression and choosing a life of humiliation rather than standing up for our dignity and honour, we resemble Yazīd's followers rather than true followers of Imam Hussein, even if we mourn and shed tears for him during the weekly and annual commemoration during Muharram.

As we know, when the captives of Karbala were presented to ibn Ziyad, the governor of Kufa, and subsequently Yazīd's court in Damascus, both the authoritarians subjected them to humiliation. They attributed the calamities and afflictions suffered by the captives to divine retribution. In the face of this, Lady Zainab eloquently declared, "I perceive nothing but beauty in the divine plan" (ibn Tawus, 1969: p. 160). Despite this declaration, regrettably, our focus on the narrative of the Imam's martyrdom and the steadfastness of his loyal companions, alongside the other gruesome atrocities committed in Karbala, has caused us to overlook the essence of the Imam's character and his noble actions. We fail to acknowledge the inherent beauty, value, and significance of his deeds, as well as the profound lessons that can be gleaned from his example to lead a virtuous life and face death with honour and dignity.

In numerous mourning ceremonies, the focus is often shifted away from the personality and character of Imam Hussein, while the crimes committed by the Yazīdis are depicted in a graphic and dramatic manner. This emphasis on emotional impact overshadows the potential for rational analysis and moral education from his life and the battle of Karbala. Thus, it is essential to highlight Imam Hussein's character, in order to recognise the extraordinary beauty of his tactical and strategic responses throughout this tragic and violent tale.[17]

4.9. Message of Imam Hussein for Our Time

Now let us see what the moral lessons of Imam Hussein for our time are. The question we should ask is this: if that honourable figure lived in the world in which we are living, what would he do in similar situations?

The goal of Imam Hussein was to combat the political injustice and reform the oppressive institutions as the most sig-

---

[17] Rumi is one of the people who, in the sixth book of Masnavi, pays attention to the beauty dimensions of this event and provides a mystical interpretation and explanation of the martyrdom of Imam Hussein.

nificant instance of injustice that needs to be fought against. It is crucial to acknowledge that injustice only makes sense when certain rights are infringed upon. Nevertheless, as is evident, the battle against political injustice encompasses various stages and conditions, with the approach adapting depending on the circumstances. Should the people not be prepared for cooperation and sacrifice, the struggle will be restricted to social activism and, at most, civil disobedience. Similarly, if corruption can be rectified through peaceful means, resorting to force and violence is impermissible. Furthermore, in cases where preserving human dignity can be accomplished by staying alive, choosing martyrdom is disallowed. Martyrdom is the act of willingly and consciously preferring death over life, and it is considered worthy only when something more valuable than life is at stake – with martyrdom being the sole means of safeguarding that superior value. As mentioned before, that superior value is nothing but human dignity.

In his influential work entitled, *Ali and the Philosophy of the Divine,* Ayatollah Ṭabāṭabā'ī sheds light on a passage from *Nahj al-Balāghah* that delves into the concept of monotheism. He asserts that: "This issue and others like it had remained unknown and unsolved in theological philosophy since its formulation, until some later Muslim philosophers [Mulla Sadra] successfully resolved it through the light of his [Imam 'Ali's] knowledge and by utilising his [Imam 'Ali's] teachings" (Ṭabātabāī, 2007: p. 317).

I believe that this claim also holds true when considering the explanation of the movement of Imam Hussein. The philosophy behind his uprising can be better comprehended by the advancements in moral philosophy since Kant's era. The principles that Imam Hussein adhered to and acted upon are not solely religious or legal standards. Rather, as espoused by Imam ʿAli and followed by Imam Hussein, they are universal moral standards. The ultimate goal was to establish a just government. The legitimacy of a political institution should be determined by fairness, rather than the religious affiliation of the ruler. Consequently, rulers can be categorised as either just or unjust, rather than Muslim or non-Muslim. Justice is a virtue that transcends religious boundaries, and religious government must conform to this criterion to gain legitimacy.

Justice cannot be divided into Islamic or non-Islamic, but Islam can be interpreted in two ways: a just interpretation (ʿAlawīte Islam) and an unjust interpretation (Umayyad Islam). ʿAlawīte Islam is characterised as a "religion within the framework of morality" and "religious governance within the framework of moral governance"; while Umayyad Islam can be described as "religion instead of morality" and "religious governance instead of moral governance". Although, when religion replaces morality, what happens in practice is that neither morality nor religion remain in place, because what takes the place of morality in actualising such a theory is not religion itself, but the will of the ruler who rules in the name of religion. In this framework, the will of the ruler becomes the source of both religion and morality.

As stated before, Imam Hussein's objective in his uprising was to establish a just government, rather than merely replacing individuals in power. His claim was that he wanted to revive the political tradition of the Prophet and Imam ʿAli.

Hence, enjoining right and forbidding wrong is not a jurisprudential duty. Rather, it is a moral, meta-religious and meta-legal duty.

In summary then, the Battle of Karbala can be best explained by highlighting two essential and justifiable ethical principles: The first is that Imam Hussein's actions were governed by the duty to struggle for political justice, with the emphasis that every individual possesses moral rights that must be upheld by societal institutions, particularly the government. When these rights are violated, it becomes the moral duty of everyone to combat the injustice. However, this struggle has its stages and levels.

Simultaneously, Imam Hussein championed the principle of human dignity, asserting that every person possesses the inherent right to live a life of respect and honour. This way of living embodies freedom and autonomy, with no external imposition. In certain circumstances, when one's existence is devoid of dignity and honour, it is preferable to choose death. These two principles served as the foundation for Imam Hussein's impassioned speeches and cause during the Battle of Karbala.

These two ethical principles are timeless, although the methods of combatting political oppression may vary depending on circumstance and time. The manifestations of these principles can also evolve over time. In modern societies, the media, political parties, and what is commonly referred to as "civil society" have a crucial role in uncovering and preventing political oppression. Likewise, ensuring that evil is not tolerated relies on the universal oversight of governmental actions.

Hence, those who advocate for justice must genuinely strive to promote true freedom and democracy. This includes establishing a strong civil society that can effectively monitor political decision-making processes and hold rulers accountable. Only through these endeavours can the claims of the advocates of justice be considered sincere.

CHAPTER FIVE

Religious and Meta-Religious Morality in Karbala

5.1. Introduction

The occasion calls for a discussion of Imam Hussein's character, the leader of the martyrs, and the most important event of his life, namely the Battle of Karbala. Much has been said about both his character and the explanation of the Battle of Karbala. Therefore, those interested in the topic know more or less about the extensive literature on it. In recent years, I have had the privilege to offer a moral explanation of the movement of Imam Hussein. Here, I do not intend to repeat that discussion. My aim is to explain a famous saying attributed to Imam Hussein: "If you do not believe in any religion and do not fear the Resurrection Day, then [at least] be free from fear and greed in your present life *(fakūnū aḥrāran fī dunyākum hadhehī)*" (ibn Ṭawus 1969: p. 120).

Imam Hussein said this to Yazīd's army in the final moments of his life, which contains important moral advice for them. However, since Imam Hussein is a moral saint whose words match his practice, one must conclude that he, before anyone else, would act according to his maxim. At first glance, his saying has a simple and clear meaning, but upon deeper analysis, it is much more profound. It speaks of salient truths which, if taken seriously, can radically change our approach towards religious knowledge and practice, giving a different colour, scent, style and context to our life. Some of those salient truths are as follows:

1. Morality has two parts: religious and meta-religious.
2. Meta-religious morality is independent of religion and religious morality.
3. Meta-religious morality precedes religion and religious morality.
4. Human motivations for moral living are diverse.
5. Meta-religious justifying and motivating reasons for action are recognised by religion.

Our discussion tonight is devoted to elaborating on these important topics.

5.2. Syntactical Structure of Imam Hussein's Saying

The Imam's saying consists of the following three sentences:

1. If you do not believe in any religion,
2. And if you do not fear the Resurrection Day,
3. Then, [at least] be free from fear and greed in your present life.

First, the syntactic structure of each sentence will be described, and then we will proceed to offer its interpretation and exposition. Forming a conditional structure, the first and third sentence function as the subordinate and the main clauses, respectively. The second sentence is a dependent clause which explains the first sentence by defining the essence of religiosity.

5.3. The Essence of Religious Life

The second sentence touches upon the essence of religiosity in Imam Hussein's eyes. According to this conception, religious life consists in the fear of being ill-fated and concerned over the afterlife, return to God, and felicity and salvation on the Resurrection Day. Religious knowledge begins with self-knowledge and Knowledge of God. However, religious life begins with the belief in the afterlife, the concern over one's fate after death, and the return to God. The question is: "Why did Imam Hussein emphasise the fear of the Resurrection Day more than the fear of God?" As an answer, we can say that the belief in the Resurrection Day takes precedence over the belief in God and the Prophet. As stated in the Qur'ān:

> "And when Allah alone is mentioned, the hearts of those who believe not in the Hereafter are repelled, and when those (whom they worship) beside Him are mentioned, behold! they are glad" (Qur'ān, 39:45).

> "And this is a blessed Scripture which we have revealed, confirming that which (was revealed) before it, that thou mayst warn the Mother of Villages and those around her. Those who believe in the Hereafter believe herein, and they are careful of their worship" (Qur'ān, 6:92).

According to the first verse above, belief in the afterlife takes precedence over belief in the Unity of God (*Tawḥīd*). The second verse states that the belief in the afterlife takes priority over the belief in the prophecy of Muhammad and in the authenticity of the Qur'ān.

5.4. Why Be Moral?

Imam Hussein's saying offers an answer to one of the most important questions in morality or moral philosophy. Concerned with the relation between moral commitment and practical reason, the question is, "Why be moral?" Humans are rational being. Therefore, they need two types of reasons for action in whatever they decide to do. Let us call them "justifying reason" and "motivating reason" respectively. The former is to convince a rational agent that doing something is right or permissible. The latter, motivates that agent to do whatever they have justifying reason to do.[18]

Concerning reasons for action, the discussion can lead to pertinent points worthy of attention, yet they are not our concern here. What is directly relevant to our discussion is that the two types of reasons for action originate from various sources, such as practical rationality, morality, religion (i.e., Sharīʿa), politics, economy, customs, the law of one's country, etc. Of these, perhaps practical rationality is the most important. By asking, *"Why be moral or why live a moral life?"*, we actually presuppose that there is a moral reason for doing or abandoning an act, and that we know what morality demands of us. Yet we would like to know whether there is a rational reason, besides the moral reason, that supports execution or abandonment of that act.

---

[18] Moral Philosophers disagree over whether the distinction between the justifying and motivating reasons is merely conceptual or the two are also distinct in their actual instances. See Rosati (2016) and Simpson (1999).

One could ask questions such as, "Is moral living reasonable and worthwhile?" or "Is observing moral values justified from the perspective of practical rationality?" In other words, the theme of these questions is whether practical rationality allows or commands us to follow ethical reasons. Therefore, the question under discussion pertains to the relationship between moral commitment and rational commitment, or morality and practical rationality.[19]

The very same questions can also be asked about the relationship between other types of reasons for action with each other, such as the relationship between religious and moral reasons. For instance, when we ask, "Why should one be religious?", we have assumed that one has some religious reasons to do something; but we actually want to know is whether "in addition to the religious, is there also a *rational* reason in favour of doing it?". In further words, "Is something that is right or permissible from a religious viewpoint also right or permissible from a rational viewpoint?"

In what follows, we focus on the relationship about the above. The importance of the question lies in the fact that living a moral life can not only inflict harm to the agent but also requires them to bear distress and hardship and to deny them joy.

According to the answer given by Imam Hussein, there are two reasons that justify performing or abandoning an act from the perspective of practical rationality. These could be fear of the Resurrection Day and recognising the intrinsic value of the act in question. As it will be elaborated, Imam

---

[19] For a detailed discussion on the relationship between ethics and practical reasoning, see Cullity and Gaut (1997).

Hussein stated that someone who is both religious and free has two rational reasons – religious and meta-religious – to live a moral life. However, someone who is not religious has only one reason, namely, the meta-religious.

From this, it becomes clear that it may be correct to insert the adverb 'at least' in the translation of the Imam's statement. The adverb is actually gives the particular meaning of the sentence originated from the conditional structure. Its use does not mean that being free is a rank lower than being religious. Instead, it means that someone who is both religious and free has two reasons for living a moral life. However, someone who is only free has just one reason. Therefore, the adverb 'at least' merely indicates the quantity of reasons rather than their quality or the ranking and value of the life based on those reasons.

5. 5. Ranks of Living a Moral Life

The Imam's third sentence – "be free in your present life" – indicates the highest and the most eminent rank of moral life, that is, moral life for the sake of morality. The moral life can be considered as having three ranks or stages that are different in terms of one's justification and motivation for living a moral life.

5.5.1. Being Moral for the Sake of Worldly Benefits

Those who occupy the first or lowest rank likely consider the personal gain or loss as the justification and motivation for living a moral life. It may be that they observe moral values, avoid usurpation, and are charitable for the sole reason of securing their own worldly interests. For example, a businessman uses the honesty to attract more customers, or a politician adheres to integrity and avoids power abuse so that they can be re-elected in the next election. Those dwelling in the lowest rank naturally display moral commitment and adhere to moral values as long as it secures their personal worldly interests. Therefore, it can be said that they have an instrumental conception of morality. They do not inflict oppression on others because they believe that the oppressor will be punished in this world. Leaving aside the worldly consequences of (un)ethical conduct, they may not have a rational justification and motivation for living a moral life.

5.5.2. Being Moral for the Sake of Eternal Salvation

Those residing in the second rank of morality view the personal gain or loss in terms of not the mundane but in the Hereafter. They too have an instrumental conception of morality. Leaving aside the otherworldly interests, they do not have a rational justification and motivation for living a moral life. Yet they would sacrifice the worldly interests for otherworldly interests, but the worldly and otherworldly loss or gain of others is important for these people as long as it related to their own worldly and otherworldly loss or gain.

These two ranks are similar in that the justification and motivation for a moral life originate from somewhere outside morality. Rationally and psychologically speaking, these people are egoists. In technical terms, it is the very economic-cum-egoistic rationality that motivates them to observe moral values. In religious terms, it is fear of loss, or greed for gain, in this world and the next.

5.5.3. Being Moral for the Sake of Morality

For those belonging to the third and highest rank of morality, the rational justification and motivation for living a moral life is derived from morality itself. These moral agents make decisions and act solely based on moral considerations rather than personal loss or gain. This is not to say that personal worldly and otherworldly loss or gain is not important for them. For someone who is rational, the personal loss or gain is essentially important. Moreover, someone who is religious, in addition to their rationality, their belief in the Afterlife prevents them from turning a blind eye to their fate after death. However, this does not play a role in their decision to live a moral life. In other words, living a moral life is essentially desirable without any instrumental desirability. Therefore, even in the absence of the loss or gain, they adhere to their moral principles.

Those residing in the third and the highest rank are not egoistic, self-centred, or in religious terms, self-worshipping. Instead, they are altruists. Their fulfilling moral duties is merely due to a sense of duty rather than the personal gain or loss. In technical terms, the practical reason that motivates them to behave morally is characterised by the altruistic rationality rather than the egoistic rationality.

The third group know there is a direct relationship between living a moral life in the present world and worldly felicity or otherworldly salvation. However, their belief in this relationship do not play a role in their living a moral life. They are free human beings because they are emancipated from the prison of fear or greed. This group most closely resembles God since God is a moral agent with purely rational justification and motivation for being moral. In the case of God, neither worldly nor otherworldly personal gain or loss can be conceived.

5.6. Moral Psychology and Types of Agents

From the perspective of Islamic moral psychology, three types of moral agents can be distinguished based on their motivating reasons for action: (1) slaves, (2) merchants, and (3) the autonomous.[20] This distinction is inspired by one of Imam ʿAli's short sayings in *Nahj al-Balāghah* (Saying no. 237). Of course, his saying concerns different types of worship or worshippers, yet his judgment seems to be generalisable to all volitional acts. It is as follows:

> Indeed, there are people who worship Allāh out of desire [for reward], and that is the worship of merchants. And there are people who worship Allāh out of fear, and that is the worship of slaves. And there are people who worship Allāh out of gratitude, and that is the worship of free people.

---

[20] By "autonomous" I refer to an agent whose motivation for performing an act stems from the intrinsic value of the act itself, rather than from fear of harmful or undesirable consequences that might result from omitting the act in this world and/or the hereafter, or from desire for beneficial and favourable outcomes for oneself in this world and/or the hereafter.

After mentioning the above saying, Majlisi also refers to another quotation by Imam 'Ali, who states:

> O my Lord, I did not worship You out of fear of Your punishment, nor out of greed for Your rewards, but I found You worthy of worship, so I worshipped You (Majlisi, 1982: 41, 14/4).

On this basis, it can be said that any action can be done for three different reasons, and by extension, the agents are also divided into three groups as to their motivations. This then leads to three types of practical rationality. Now, if we apply this threefold taxonomy to the realm of morality, we will arrive at three types of moral commitment, which may not differ much in terms of the external behaviour as they may possess similar axiological or normative system. For example, something that is wrong is wrong for all. Yet the three kinds of moral commitment differ from one another in terms of motivating reasons for action. Therefore, the people who lead a moral life can be classified into three groups:

1. Those who are moral out of *fear* of the undesirable consequences of being immoral or amoral.
2. Those who are moral out of *greed* for the expected rewards for being moral, and
3. Those who are moral because being moral is *intrinsically* good.

5.6.1. The Moral Psychology of Slaves

Slaves' morality is based on the *fear* of worldly or otherworldly consequences of being immoral or amoral. That is, those who have a slavish psychological makeup cannot be rationally convinced, nor can they be psychologically motivated by any reason, except by those that are based on fear of the bad consequences of their immoral or amoral actions. Therefore, in the absence of fear-based reasons for action, moral reasons alone are insufficient or too weak to motivate them.

5.6.2. The Moral Psychology of Merchants

Merchants' morality is based on calculating personal gain and loss, or cost-benefit analysis. This can also be worldly and/or otherworldly. In this case, the consideration of profit and loss provides both justifying and motivating reasons for being moral for the merchant-minded agents. Therefore, in the absence of greed, moral reasons alone will not be able to justify and motivate them.

5.6.3. The Moral Psychology of Autonomous Agents

Autonomous agents are those who have *inner* freedom, which is totally different from *outer* freedom. They are called "the liberated" (*aḥrār*) in our religious literature. The "liberated" or "autonomous" person differs from the "free" person, just as "inner freedom" differs from "outer freedom". Outer freedom means: "emancipation from *external* constraints and limitations imposed by others on the individual". But inner freedom means "emancipation from *internal* constraints and limitations imposed by one's own psychological make up on oneself". In other words, inner freedom means "emancipation from fear and greed". Therefore, one may have outer freedom without having inner freedom, and vice versa. This type of moral life can be called "moral living for the sake of morality".

The morality of the autonomous agents is not based on fear and greed but stems from appreciating the intrinsic value of moral life. For someone who has inner freedom, moral reasons alone suffice to both justify and motivate them to be moral.

5.7. The Status of Freedom in the Modern and Pre-Modern World

One of the fundamental differences between the modern and pre-modern world has to do with the dominant conception of freedom. In the premodern world, the main emphasis was on inner freedom, while outer freedom was either unimportant or secondary. But in the modern world, the opposite seems to be true. In this era, external freedom is emphasised as a fundamental value, yet there is no discourse regarding inner freedom and its value and importance. Perhaps the reason for this is that if inner freedom were to be added to external freedom, the interests of the wealthy (the unbridled capitalist system) and the powerful (totalitarian political systems) would be endangered.

The important point to consider here is that outer freedom without inner freedom does not alleviate human suffering, although someone who has outer freedom is better off than someone who has neither outer nor inner freedom. In other words, having inner freedom does not fill the void of outer freedom, and vice versa. However, it is also undeniable that as long as a person is inwardly captive to fear and greed, externally they are prone to exploitation by others; and thus, others can indirectly and imperceptibly deprive or limit the person's (outer) freedom by playing on their fear or greed; that is, make decisions instead of him and determine his fate.

The illusion of freedom differs from real freedom. Outer freedom without inner freedom is merely the illusion of freedom. For, as long as a person remains captive to fear and greed, others will be able to manipulate them through these channels, compelling them to willingly pursue others' objectives and serve their interests while deluding themselves that they have decided freely rather than having decisions made for them. This does not imply that outer freedom is not important, but rather that the genuine realisation of outer freedom is contingent upon inner freedom. Freedom is a value that cannot be achieved merely by liberation from external constraints; it additionally depends on emancipation from internal constraints (fear and greed). I think, when Imanuel Kant defines "rational agency" in terms of "autonomy", what he meant is not just having outer freedom; rather, he also meant a combination of outer and inner freedoms.[21]

At this point, another important difference can be observed between the modern and the pre-modern world. Many of the common moral abnormalities in the pre-modern world have not disappeared with the advent of modernity, but have taken on a different form: from being overt/hard to covert/soft. As an example, let us consider slavery. Some-

---

[21] For the notion of rational agency and its relation to freedom and autonomy in Kant's moral philosophy, see (Allison 1990). Also, for the historical origin of the notion of autonomy and its centrality in modern moral philosophy, see (Schneewind 1998).

one seeking to enslave others may employ overt force and achieve their goal by depriving people of their external freedom. This method was common in the pre-modern world.

Yet, the same person may recognise the external freedom of others and not impose anything on them by naked force, but play on their inner vulnerabilities, such as fear and greed, and allure them into 'willingly' choosing slavery; thus, making them give up their outer freedom in return for meeting their contingent desires and avoiding contingent harms. This is the prevailing form of slavery in the modern world. Therefore, through manipulating desires and fears, modern slavery traps people inwardly rather than directly restricting them outwardly.

5.8. The Interpretation of Imam Hussein's Saying

Now in light of these explanations, let us return to Imam Hussein's statement, in which he criticises the behaviour of Yazīd's army and invites them to reflect on their behaviour and revise their conduct. Obviously, his criticism is universal and not specific to this particular case, so it is applicable to all immoral conducts. This is why his saying is of utmost importance and relevance for us as we can use it to address anyone whose behaviour towards others is immoral, such as someone who lies to others, violates the rights of others, does not keep his promises, backbites about others, displays indifference to the suffering of others, does not help the needy, and steals or embezzles. Addressing such a person, we can say, "If you do not believe in religion and do not fear the Resurrection Day, at least be autonomous in your worldly life."

5.8.1. Imam Hussein's Insights into Diagnosing Moral Disorders

This saying of Imam Hussein is based on a kind of "moral pathology", according to which all immoral behaviours stem from two things: one is the lack of concern about one's fate after death, and the other is the lack of inner freedom. If someone lacks both of these two sources of motivation, they will not have the necessary foundation for being moral.

In other words, in the moral psychology that is inferred from religious texts, including this saying of Imam Hussein, the two biggest obstacles for being moral are fear and greed. If one looks at the Qur'ānic verses from this angle, it will be clearly observed that according to the Qur'ān, Satan and his army deceive people in two different ways: either through fear or through greed (see for example, Qur'ān, 2:268 and 7:22-20). The mechanism of self-deception is also based on the lack of inner freedom. That is, when people deceive themselves, they manipulate their own reason by exploiting their fears and desires.

5.8.2. The Role of Religion in the Domain of Morality

If someone says to others, "If you do not believe in any religion, at least be autonomous", he has accepted the view that it is possible to be moral without religion, which implies the recognition of the rational-cum-psychological independence of morality from religion.

If the required justification and motivation for being moral can be stemmed from outside of religion, the question thus arises concerning the role of religion in moral knowledge and practice. The answer to this question is so detailed that it cannot be fully dealt with here. To put it succinctly, religion can play an important role in the moral growth or moral decline of its followers. Which of these two roles religion actually plays depends on whether followers properly understand and act on religious teachings. Religious education can both cultivate the moral conscience of human beings or diminish, suppress or distort it.

In other words, the constructive or destructive role of religion in the domain of moral life depends on having the right or wrong understanding of the relationship between religion and morality. If one embraces the view that morality takes precedence over religion, then their religious knowledge and practice will have a moral framework, and religion will help its followers to become moral and remain so. However, if believers' position on the relationship between religion and morality is that religion precedes or substitutes morality, then they will err both in understanding religion and in following it; and such a incorrect understanding will also corrupt their moral life.

5.8.3. The Role of Religion in Moral Development

Moreover, religion can gradually free humans from the shackles of fear and greed and lead them to the state of being autonomous. Specifically, there are three important religious teachings that play a significant role in this respect:

1. The moral order of the universe

2. The Afterlife
3. *Tawḥīd* in practice or monotheism in worship

These teachings operate in three stages. In the first stage, religion tries to persuade its followers that the order governing the world in which humans live is not only natural-cum-scientific but also moral. As Rumi says, "This world is the mountain, and our action the shout; the echo of the shout comes [back] to us,", or as Saʿdī says, "Do good and throw something in the river; one day God will bring it back to you in the desert". This implies the necessity of first acknowledging the existence of fear and greed in human nature. Being realistic in moral education requires us to acknowledge the existence of fear and greed as sources of motivation in the first stage, but trying to convince them that following moral reasons plays a role in averting what they fear and attaining what they desire.

In the second stage, religion strives to redirect the fear and greed of its followers from this world towards the Hereafter; that is, to change the subject of fear and greed or expand their domain. In these two stages, it is not necessary to ask people to replace their sources of motivation in order to be moral, for indeed it is very difficult if not impossible, especially for those who are at the cusp of their moral journey. Instead, suffice it to convince them that: (1) a moral order governs the universe, and (2) death is not the end but the beginning of an eternal life.

At the third stage, religion strives to replace *self-centredness* with *God-centredness*. Fear and greed stem from self-centeredness. Therefore, if humans change their orientation in life by replacing self-centeredness with God-centeredness, the weakness mentioned before will naturally be eliminated. Those servants of God who worship Him for His own sake rather than out of greed for heaven or the fear of hell, are the freest beings in the world, for such spiritual practice enables them to attain the station of autonomy or inner freedom. The inner voice of one who reaches such a station is: "Since the day I submitted to You, I became free." Of course, all these personality transformations are contingent upon having a proper conception of the nature of God, religion and morality, as well as of the relationship of these conceptions with one another. The God that such people worship must be a moral agent, not a tyrant, and they must worship such a God for His own sake.

5.8.4 Morality as a Meta-religious Category

Recognising the independence of morality from religion is tantamount to accepting the claim that morality is a "meta-religious" category. When Imam Hussein says to his enemies, "If you do not have a religion, at least be internally free", he argues with them based on a meta-religious grounds. In other words, the Imam is saying that in order to judge who is righteous, one does not need to be religious; possessing inner freedom is sufficient for the purpose.

5.8.5. Religion and Morality in the Realm of Politics

Another important point that can be inferred from the saying of Imam Hussein is this: Given that the interaction of the two combating groups in Karbala was political in nature, it can be said that someone who argues this way with his enemies and invites them to be autonomous in their political conduct, has assumed the existence of a kind of political morality based on inner freedom and its independence from religion. This is, I think, the plausible meaning of the separation of politics from religion. Separating religion from politics does not mean that religion plays no role, or should not play a role, in politics. Rather it means that religion's intervention in politics has a moral framework, and religious law cannot and should not replace moral law in the realm of politics. Imam Hussein's political position was more ethical than religious, and for reasons previously explained, he was more concerned with establishing a moral government based on meta-religious morality rather than establishing a religious government outside of the moral framework.

5.8.6. Karbala: A Battle between Inner Freedom with Fear and Greed

Finally, the last point I would like to emphasise in interpreting this saying of Imam Hussein is that someone who sincerely invites others to be liberated from the shackles of fear and greed, has already liberated himself. Therefore, true lovers and sincere followers of Imam Hussein are those who have cultivated that true freedom within their own souls.

Karbala symbolises a battleground where fear and greed clash with inner freedom. This is why it can be said: "Every land is Karbala, and every day is Ashura", as this battle will continue for as long as there are human beings living on earth. If our love for Imam Hussein and commemoration of his martyrdom fail to liberate us from the prison of fear and greed, then it would be clear that either we do not truly understand Imam Hussein or our admiration and expressions of love for him are dishonest – or at least, underdeveloped. The month of Muharram in particular offers a valuable opportunity for each of us to self-reflect and by examining our inner state, to be our own judge as to which side of the battle we find ourselves aligned with.

In summary, the battlefield of Karbala serves as a stage for the confrontation between two forms of religious knowledge and practice: one being the Umayyad way of life, characterised by fear of authority and worldly loss, and greed for worldly gain; and the other, the 'Alawīte way of life, founded upon inner freedom.

REFERENCES

Abu Mikḥnaf al-Kufi, L. (1996/1417 AH) *Waqʿat al-Ṭaff*, (Qom: Jamʿiyyat al-Mudarrisīn).

Acton, J. (1887) Letter on Historical Integrity.

Allison, H. E. (1990). *Kant's Theory of Freedom.* (Cambridge: Cambridge University Press).

al-Māwardī, A. L. H. (2018). *Al-Ahkam As-Sultaniyyah: The Laws of Islamic Governance.* (Beyrut: Dar Ul Thaqafah).

Arbilī, ʿA. (2002/1381 AH) *Kashf al-Ghummah Fī Maʿrifat al-Aʾimmah*, (Tabriz: Intisharat Banī Hāshim).

Arendt, H. (1970) *On Violence.* (Eugene: Harvest Books).

Assmann, J. (2018). "Monotheism–Curse or Blessing?", in Pirner, M. L. et al. (eds.) *Public Theology, Religious Diversity, and Interreligious Learning*, 94-104. (New York: Rutledge).

Cook, D. (2007). *Martyrdom in Islam.* (Cambridge: Cambridge University Press).

Cullity, G., & Gaut, B. (eds.) (1997) *Ethics and Practical Reason* (Oxford: Clarendon Press).

Fanāʾī, F. (2005/1384 AH) *Dīn dar Tárāzū-ye Akhlāq*, (Tehran: Intisharat Ṣirāṭ).

Han, B. C. (2018). *Topology of Violence.* (Boston, MIT Press).

Harʿāmallāhī, M. (1988/1409 AH) *Tafsīl Wasaʾil al-Shīʿah Ila Taḥsīl Masāʾil al-Sharīʿah*, (Qom: Muʾassasat Ahl al-Bayt ʿAlayhim al-Salām).

Hedāyatpánāh, M. (2009/1388 AH) Bāztabl Taʿammul-i ʿUthmānī dar Wāqiʾah-yi Karbalāʾ (Qom: Púyeshkade-ye Ḥuze va Dāneshgāh).

Ibn Shuʿbah al-Harrani, H. (1943/1363 AH) *Tuḥaf al-ʿUqūl* (Qom: Intisharat Jamʿiyyat al-Mudarrisīn).

Ibn Ṭawūs, 'A. (1969/1348 AH) *al-Lāhūf 'Alá Qatlá al-Ṭufūf,* translated by Aḥmad Fahri Zanjani, (Tehran: Intisharat Jahan).

Kant, I. (1999) *Practical Philosophy,* Mary Gregor (Trans.), (Cambridge University Press).

Kulaynī, M. (1986/1407 AH) *al-Kāfī,* (Tehran: Dār al-Kutub al-Islāmiyyah).

Majlisī, M. (1982/1403 AH) *Biḥār al-Anwār al-Jāmi'ah li-Durar Akbār al-A'immat al-Aṭhār,* (Beirut: Dār Iḥyā' al-Turāth al-'Arabī).

Majlisī, M. (1985/1406 AH) *Maladh al-Akhhyār Fī Fahm Tahdhīb al-Akhbār,* (Qom: Ketābkhāneh Ayat Allāh Mar'ashī Najafī).

Muṭahharī, M. (1998/1377 AH) *Ḥamāse-ye Ḥusaynī, Majmū'e-ye Āthār Ostād Sheykh Muṭahharī,* (Tehran: Intisharat Ṣadrā), Vol. 17.

Menqarī, N. (1983/1404 AH) *Waq'at al-Ṣiffīn,* (Qom: Maktabat Ayatullah Mar'ashī Najafī).

Mufīd, M. (1992/1413 AH) *al-Irshād Fī Ma'rifat Ḥujjat Allāh 'Alá al-'Ibād,* (Qom: Kongoreh Sheykh Mufīd).

Rayy Shahrī, M. et al. (2006/1427 AH) *Mawsu'at al-Imām 'Alī ibn Abī Ṭālib Fī al-Kitāb wa al-Sunnah wa al-Tārīkh,* (Qom: Dār al-Ḥadīth).

Rosati, C. S. (2016) "Moral Motivation", *Stanford Encyclopedia of Philosophy.*

Sayyid Raḍī, M. (1993/1414 AH) *Nahj al-Balāghah,* Taḥqīq Ṣabḥī Ṣāliḥ, (Qom: Intisharat Hijrat).

Schneewind, J. B. (1998). *The Invention of Autonomy: A History of Modern Moral Philosophy.* (Cambridge: Cambridge University Press).

Simā'ī, M. (2018/1397 AH) *Mashhūrāt Bī-I'tibār dar Tārīkh wa Ḥadīth*, (Qom: Intisharat Ṭāhah).

Shari'atī, 'A. (1988/1367) *Ḥusayn Wārith Ādam: Majmū'ah Āthār Duktūr Shari'atī* (Tehran: Intisharat Qalam), J. 19.

Ṣāliḥī Najafābādī, N. (1970/1349 AH) *Shahīd Jāwīd* (Tehran: Intisharat Mash'al Āzādī).

Ṣadr al-Dīn al-Shīrāzī, M. (2004/1383 AH) *Sharḥ Uṣūl al-Kāfī*, (Tehran: Mu'assasat Mutāla'āt wa Taḥqīqāt al-Farhangī).

Simpson, E. (1999) "Between Internalism and Externalism in Ethics", *The Philosophical Quarterly*, 49 (195), 201-214.

Soroush, 'A. (2008). "Essentials and Accidentals in Religion", in his *The Expansion of Prophetic Experience: Essays on Historicity, Contingency and Plurality in Religion*. Brill, chapter 4.

Soroush, 'A. (2000/1379) "Ḥusayn b. 'Alī wa Jalāl al-Dīn Rūmī", *Qamar-i 'Āshiqānah*, (Tehran: Intisharat Ṣirāṭ), pp. 139-165.

Ṭabarī, F. (1982/1403 AH) *al-Iḥtijāj 'Alá Ahl al-Lijāj*, (Mashhad: Nashr Murtadhá).

Ṭabāṭabā'ī, S. M. (2007/1428 AH) "'Alī wa al-Falsafah al-Ilāhi-yyah", *al-Insān wa al-I'tiqād* (Qom: al-Bāqiyāt), pp. 277-336.

Tamimi Amadi, 'A. (1989/1410 AH) *Ghurar al-Ḥikam wa Durar al-Kalim*, (Qom: Dār al-Kutub al-Islāmiyyah).

Wadell, C. P., & Paul, J. (1990). *Friendship and the Moral Life*. (Notre Dame: University of Notre Dame Pess).

Žižek, S. (2008) *Violence: Six Sideways Reflection*. (London: Profile Books).